LAPSING OUT

LAPSING OUT

Embodiments of Death and Rebirth
in the Last Writings
of D. H. LAWRENCE

Donald Gutierrez

RUTHERFORD • MADISON • TEANECK
FAIRLEIGH DICKINSON UNIVERSITY PRESS
LONDON AND TORONTO: ASSOCIATED UNIVERSITY PRESSES

©1980 by Associated University Presses, Inc.

Associated University Presses, Inc.
Cranbury, New Jersey 08512

Associated University Presses
Magdalen House
136-148 Tooley Street
London SE1 2TT, England

Associated University Presses
Toronto M5E 1A7, Canada

Library of Congress Cataloging in Publication Data

Gutierrez, Donald.
    Lapsing out.

    Bibliography: p.
    Includes index.

    1. Lawrence, David Herbert, 1885-1930—Criticism and interpretation. 2. Death in literature. 3. Regeneration in literature. I. Title.
PR6023.A93Z63114   1980   823'.9'12   78-75177
ISBN 0-8386-2293-3

Printed in the United States of America

You've got to lapse out before you can know what sensual reality is, lapse into unknowingness, and give up your volition. . . .You've got to learn not-to-be, before you can come into being.
—D. H. Lawrence, *Women in Love*

Rise. . .men of the Risen Lord, and push back the stone. Who rises with the risen lord rises himself as a lord.
—D. H. Lawrence, *Phoenix*

. . .he died, saying, "I never felt better in my life."
—Malcolm Lowry, *Hear Us O Lord From Heaven Thy Dwelling Place*

Newness is renewal. . .making it new again. . . .Reformation vs. renaissance; rebirth. Life is Phoenix-like, always being born again out of its own death. The true nature of life is resurrection; all life is life after death, a second life, reincarnation.
—Norman O. Brown, *Love's Body*

When we postulate a beginning, we only do so to fix a starting point for our thought. There never was a beginning, and there never will be an end of the universe.
—D. H. Lawrence, *The Symbolic Meaning*

Death is destroyer and redeemer; it is the ultimate cruelty andd the essence of release. . . .Although undeniably ubiquitous, death is incomprehensibly unique.
—Edwin S. Shneidman, *Deaths of Man*

Grave men, near death, who see with blinding sight
Blind eyes could blaze like meteors and be gay,
Rage, rage against the dying of the light.
—Dylan Thomas, "Do Not Go Gentle into that Good Night"

A man's birth is an uncontrolled event in his life, but the manner of his departure from life bears a definite relation to his philosophy of life and death. We are mistaken to consider death as a purely biological event. The attitudes concerning it and its meaning for the individual can serve as an important organizing principle in determining how he conducts himself in life.
—Herman Feifel, *The Meaning of Death*

... immortality is in the vividness of life, not in the loss of life.
—D. H. Lawrence, *Phoenix*

That which is understood by man is surpassed by man. When we understand our extreme being in death, we have surpassed into a new being.
—D. H. Lawrence "The Reality of Peace," *Phoenix*

To Marlene

Contents

Acknowledgments	11
1 Introduction	15
2 Lapsing Out: Ideas of Mortality and Immortality in Lawrence	27
3 *The Virgin and the Gipsy* as Ironic Comedy	55
4 D. H. Lawrence's Golden Age	68
5 Circles and Arcs: The Rhythm of Circularity and Centrifugality in *Last Poems*	118
6 "A New Haven and an Old Earth:" Lawrence's *Apocalypse*, Apocalyptic, and the *Book of Revelation*	129
Conclusion	168
Selected Bibliography	172
Index	179

Acknowledgments

I wish to thank the following publishers and journals for having given me permission to quote from published works:

The Bobbs-Merrill Company, Inc., for permission to quote W. H. Davies' "Leisure" from *English Poetry in Transition: 1880-1920* (1968).

The D. H. Lawrence Review, for permission to reprint my articles "Circles and Arcs: The Rhythm of Circularity and Centrifugality in D. H. Lawrence's *Last Poems*, vol. 4, no. 3 (Fall 1971), and "D. H. Lawrence's Golden Age," vol. 9, no. 3 (Fall 1976).

Laurence Pollinger, Ltd., and the Estate of the late Mrs. Frieda Lawrence Ravagli, for permission to quote from D. H. Lawrence, *The Complete Poems of D. H. Lawrence*, ed. by Vivian de Sola Pinto and F. Warren Roberts (1964, 1971); D. H. Lawrence, *Sons and Lovers* (1958); D. H. Lawrence, *The Rainbow* (1961); D. H. Lawrence, *Lawrence and Italy* (1972); D.H. Lawrence, *Phoenix II*, ed. by F. Warren Roberts and Harry T. Moore (1972); D. H. Lawrence, *The Symbolic Meaning: The Uncollected Versions of Studies of Classic American Literature* (1964).

Lewis S. Feuer, for permission to quote from Lewis S. Feuer, ed., *Basic Writings in Political Philosophy: Karl Marx and Friedrich Engels* (1958).

The MacMillan Company of Canada Limited for permission to quote from Miguel de Cervantes, *Don Quixote* (1964).

Oxford University Press for permission to quote from Norman Cohn, *The Pursuit of the Millenium* (1957).

Random House, Inc., and Alfred A. Knopf, Inc., for permission to quote from D. H. Lawrence, *The Virgin and the Gipsy* (1930, 1968).

Review of Existential Psychology & Psychiatry, for permission to reprint my article "A New Heaven and An Old Earth: D. H. Lawrence's *Apocalpyse*, Apocalpytic, and The *Book of Revelation*, vol. 15, no. 1 (1977).

Twentieth Century Literature, for permission to reprint my article "Lapsing Out: Ideas of Mortality and Immortality in Lawrence," vol. 24, no. 2 (Summer 1978).

The Viking Press, Inc., for permission to quote from D. H. Lawrence, *The Complete Poems of D. H. Lawrence*, ed. by Vivian de Sola Pinto and F. Warren Roberts (1964, 1971); D. H. Lawrence, *Sons and Lovers* (1958); D. H. Lawrence, *The Rainbow* (1961); D. H. Lawrence, *Lawrence and Italy* (1972); D. H. Lawrence *Phoenix II*, ed. by F. Warren Roberts and Harry T. Moore (1972); D. H. Lawrence, *The Symbolic Meaning: The Uncollected Versions of Studies of Classic American Literature* (1964).

In addition, I would like to convey special thanks to the following scholars and friends who, whether directly or indirectly, have helped to make this book possible: Professors L. D. Clark, James C. Cowan, John Jenkins Espey, Martin Green, Leo Hamalian, and Kingsley Widmer. I am also indebted to Western New Mexico University for giving me a job in academically hard times as well as summer-grants support essential to my pursuing research activities.

LAPSING OUT

1
Introduction

I

In a hortatory essay called "Resurrection," written early in 1925 shortly after suffering a grave illness in Oaxaca, Mexico, D. H. Lawrence wrote as follows:

> Now, as Christians, we have died. The War was the Calvary of all real Christian men. Since the War, it has been the tomb, with no rule at all. . . .
> Rise as the Lord. No longer the man of sorrows. The Crucified uncrucified. The Crown of Thorns removed, and the tongues of fire round the brows. The Risen Lord. . . .
> Put away the Cross; it is obsolete. Stare no more after the Stigmata. They are more than healed up. The Lord is risen, and ascended unto the Father. There is a new body, and a new Law. . . .
> Men who can rise with the Son of Man, and ascend unto the Father, will see the new day. Many men will perish in the tomb, unable to roll the stone away. ["Resurrection" in *Phoenix*, pp. 737-38]

Whether or not this is an accurate description of man's spiritual condition following World War I, this brief essay-sermon accurately registers Lawrence's mind at the time. The cast of mind—apocalyptical and resurrectionary—markedly characterizes Lawrence's last years of work. But Lawrence throughout much of his career was prone to this kind of thinking, partly because of his physical condition. Aldous Huxley once said that "For Lawrence, existence was a continuous convalescence; it was as though he were newly reborn from a mortal illness every day of his life."[1] George H. Ford buttresses this observation by stating that "in Lawrence's case it is evident that these severe illnesses permanently affected his appreciation of daily living . . ."[2] Lawrence responded to life with the acuity of a man given an indefinite but limited time in which to live. Thus in Lawrence intensity compensated for quantity, and his sensibility of vitalism he crystallized in his art.

Lawrence underwent at least four "deaths" in his lifetime. According to Professor Ford, "The pneumonia which attacked him when he was 17 and again when he was 26 was so severe that on both occasions he was almost given up for dead."[3] The first near-death is memorably duplicated in *Sons and Lovers* as Paul Morel's serious illness that occurs shortly after the oldest brother William dies. It is known that the first two "deaths" correspond to crucial changes in Lawrence's relationship with his mother. The first change concerned his rejection by his mother after the death of Ernest (the William of the novel), and the second occurred when his mother died, a period described with terrifying vividness in the final chapters of *Sons and Lovers*. The First World War, which "put a spear" through Lawrence-Christ, is properly identified as a death laden with portentous futurity.[4] That the war was also the death of Lawrence's significant work after *Women in Love* is a notion that we in turn will attempt to put to rest.[5]

The fourth time Lawrence nearly died was in February 1925 while residing in Oaxaca, Mexico, when he came down with tuberculosis.[6] According to L. D. Clark, "Lawrence began to suffer in Oaxaca, before he had finished writing *The Plumed Serpent*, the worst illness he had ever experienced [p. 46] . . . the illness . . . was so severe that for a few days he despaired of recovery."[7] Associated with this period besides "Resurrection" is another short work bearing eschatological elements derived from Lawrence's illness. Entitled "The Flying Fish," this fictional fragment is a key work because it opens a gateway to the pronounced apocalyptical and death-and-rebirth concerns of Lawrence's last work. Indeed, "The Flying Fish" can be used to demarcate the works of 1926-1930 as a distinct section of the Lawrence canon. That this period has already been sectioned off in comprehensive critical and biographical books on Lawrence (not to mention specialized or generic studies) provides some authority for such periodizing.[8]

But further evidence for this division is available, particularly if we look more closely at specific works of the last years. The point, however, is to validate the autonomy of this portion of the canon on the strength of its own character and worth. The Lawrence who almost died in the mid-1920s after the dubious leadership novels and the splendid short fiction and fauna-and-flora poems, was in fact "resurrected" into another and final life of creativity, strikingly different in interests and disposition from the leader-follower theses of the post war works, and from the preceding periods as well. By dealing at length and from a central perspective with major writings from these last years of Lawrence's output, I hope to add to the little work done so far to validate the periodic integrity of the post-1925 phase, and, more important, its imaginative excellence.

II

In 1925 Lawrence told his New England friends Earl and Achsah Brewster that he did not finish "The Flying Fish" because it "was written too near the borderline of death" to be completed during the subsequent period of recovery.[9] He also told them that "the last part will be [about] regenerate man, a real life in the Garden of Eden," "a plan," says James C. Cowan, "which was realized in part, in a somewhat different version, in *The Man Who Died*."[10] But this concept and ideal of the "regenerate man" (and woman) is dramatized in Lawrence's "late" period generally in works like *Lady Chatterley's Lover, Etruscan Places, Last Poems*, and in the comic initiation ritual of *The Virgin and the Gipsy* and the iconoclastic vision of *Apocalypse*.

Professor Cowan supplies a valuable lead in defining the character of this late period (and of "The Flying Fish" specifically) as a matrix for the reorientation of Lawrence's interests and creative energies toward death and rebirth: "Lawrence's serious illness of the Winter of 1925 was perhaps his deepest descent into his own primordial unconscious, lying deeper than sex, beyond sex, where the ultimate distinction is between life and death. Yet, as Joseph Campbell says of the monomythic hero: "His consciousness having succumbed, the unconsciousness nevertheless supplies its own balance, and he is born back into the world from which he came. Instead of holding to and saving his ego, . . . he loses it, and yet, through grace, it is returned."[11]

However, Lawrence's revivification during this time, surpassing sex in its sweep, also includes sex, as works like *Lady Chatterley's Lover, The Virgin and the Gipsy*, and *The Man Who Died* attest. But sex now more vividly symbolizes the new surge in Lawrence toward a "second life," rather than the esoterically manipulated medium in Lawrence's great novels of the 1910s by which the recesses of character were explored. David Cavitch has a psychoanalytical interpretation of "The Flying Fish" relevant to this critical point of release for Lawrence into a new phase of creative sensibility: "The change in Lawrence's unconscious appears [in "The Flying Fish"] in his delight with the symbols of ocean, fish, and porpoises—which are transformations of his recent images of dread, such as his deadly mountains [*The Princess, The Woman Who Rode Away*], his feathered snake [*The Plumed Serpent*] and fiery stallion [*St. Mawr*]."[12] Professor Cavitch also identifies a kind of matricidal misogyny in Lawrence's writings from *Sons and Lovers* to "The Flying Fish" (including the death in this story of the motherly sister of the Lawrence protagonist, Gethin Day, who is named Lydia—the name of Lawrence's mother), which, according to Cavitch, liberated Lawrence from maternal captivity.[13] If this idea is correct, it might also explain in part the bold, overt treatment of sexuality found in such late fictions as *The Man Who Died* and *Lady Chatterley's Lover*, in the powerful ideologically sexual formulations of three famous essays of the period: "A Propos of *Lady Chatterley's Lover*," "Introduction to His Paintings," and "Pornography and Obscenity," and in more than a few poems in the late collection of verses called *Pansies*.

One exciting rebirth motif in writings of this period appears prototypically in the following passage from "The Flying Fish" when Gethin Day, on his trip back to Daybrook and his own "rebirth" of integration, watches a school of dolphins in the Caribbean cavorting alongside the ship:

> They gave off into the water their marvellous joy of life, such as the man had never met before. And it left him wonderstruck. 'But they know joy, they know pure joy!' he said to himself in amazement. 'This is the most laughing joy I have ever seen, pure and unmixed. . . . Men have not got in them that secret to be alive together and make one like a single laugh, yet each fish going his own gait. This is sheer joy—and men have lost it. . . . the togetherness of love is nothing to the spinning unison of dolphins playing undersea. It would be wonderful to know joy as these fish know it. The life of the deep waters is ahead of us, it contains sheer togetherness and sheer joy. We have never got there.' [*Phoenix*, pp. 794-95]

Not all of the final writings are immersed in this "prelapsarian joy anterior to self-consciousness," as Cowan has phrased it, but this joy possibly functioned as an impetus and organizing energy for some of them. Transformations of this fishy jubilance also appear as motifs of major significance in the ritualistic celebratory dancing, flower-decorating, and sexual commingling in *Lady Chatterley's Lover*, the happy awe of the reborn "Man's" discovery of his erotic potency in *The Man Who Died*, and the gaily graceful dancing-and-banqueting Etruscans in *Etruscan Places*. The joy prefigured in "The Flying Fish" offers in its intimations of a communal Eden and a watery future arresting metaphors for the "sea change' of death and rebirth in the last writings.

III

The major works of the last period are *The Virgin and the Gypsy, Etruscan Places, Lady Chatterley's Lover, The Man Who Died, Last Poems,* and *Apocalypse* (such essays of this phase as "Pornography and Obscenity," "Introduction to His Paintings," and "A Propos of *Lady Chatterley's Lover,*" important credal statements, will be related briefly to our governing theme). None of this material has received critical or interpretive treatment *en bloc*, as an organic unit of work. Such treatment (excluding *Lady Chatterley's Lover*) is the intention of this study. Although *Last Poems* and *The Man Who Died* have been given critical attention separately, they have not been scrutinized together from a large controlling perspective. The other works—*Etruscan Places, Apocalypse,* and *The Virgin and the Gipsy*—have gone almost unnoticed by literary scholars.[14]

My plan then is to approach this body and period of writing through the idea central to Lawrence's work of death and rebirth. Lawrence, as the reader knows, continually improvised on this theme, but fundamentally he used it as a paradigm and test on the one hand of egoistic hyperconsciousness and self-consciousness (that he regarded as a kind of death-in-life). The polarized antithesis to this state of being Lawrence regarded as an ego-transcendence into a condition of enhanced being.

Distinctive in Lawrence's last works is a tendency to relate death-and-rebirth conceptions to biological death. This activity can be observed on the individual level of the Lawrence persona in many of the last poems, as a physical-mythical death and rebirth in *The Man Who Died*, and on an extended, societal basis in the last "travel" book *Etruscan Places* in which a dead society is revivified. It assumes finally the courageous aspect in *Apocalypse* of an antiapocalyptic, a position attacking immortality as deific revenge and chiliastic utopianism.

An objection that could be made to the last-phase periodization proposed in this book is that death-and-rebirth elements pervade much of Lawrence's work. This is not a valid stricture if one keeps in mind the enlarging pressure upon Lawrence during his final five years of his own biological death. To his other uses of "dissolution" and regeneration is added, with high gains in irony, pathos, mysticism, and ambiguity, the increasing certainty and specificity of physical death.

In Chapter 2, I discuss the idea of death and rebirth as it figures in some of the pivotal works of the Lawrence canon. This enterprise has two purposes: to indicate the extent to which Lawrence's work is generally immersed in eschatological thinking, and to examine some of the forms his eschatology takes (which should help to differentiate these elements in the work prior to the last period, and in the last period.)

Such a differentiation is not easily made; implications Lawrence achieved in his better work could transcend such categorizing as figurative death and literal death. A thesis underlying this study is that the quality of transfiguration in the last works acquires added artistic, philosophic, and religious distinction if we perceive their thanatological dimension. A basic concern in thantology, the study of death and dying, is stated by the thanatologist Edwin S. Shneidman in his book *Deaths of Man*: "One key question is how one [who is dying] makes the transition from . . . negative affective states . . . to a state of acceptance" (p. 6). In works like *Last Poems* Lawrence dramatizes this consideration in meditations upon authenticity of being and nonbeing during the process of dying; he does so in other works of the period by placing literal and figurative death in the context of images and conceptions of, and forces against, resurrection. Lawrence's own experience of daily rebirth induced by his tubercular condition resembles what the thanatologists call a "postmortem life" or what John Keats termed a "posthumous existence."[15] In a sense going beyond punning, this last phase might aptly be described as the posthumous Lawrence.

The idea of a comic resurrection has its place in a writer treating of death with such rich ambiguity. Chapter 4 accordinly presents the novella *The Virgin and the Gipsy* as ironic comedy and as a rite of passage of youth to the threshold of adulthood. This chapter, aside from its comedic focus, is the only one in the study dealing at length with rebirth in youth. "Death" in this context becomes the relinquishment of youth and the virginal sensibility through sexual awakening. *"Dolphin"* joy translates into a girl's movement towards womanly self-awareness.

The two books that comprise the center of this study, *Etruscan Places* and *Apocalypse*, although largely ignored by critics, are not only important in their own right in any general assessment of Lawrence, but, from the perspective being implemented in this book, represent indispensable if figurative examples of death and rebirth. *Etruscan Places* reveals Lawrence's resurrecting a buried and mysterious ancient people and "burying" a "dead" one, the mechanistic Romans; *Apocalypse*, Lawrence's last book, presents an iconoclastic interpretation of the *Book of Revelation*.

Etruscan Places depicts a people who almost embody Lawrence's "momentaneity" poetic in his "Preface to New Poems": ". . . free verse is, or should be . . . the soul and body and mind surging at once, nothing left out. . . . we speak of the instant, the immediate self, the very plasm of the self." This

"Italian" book, so lively, so vivaciously alert one feels almost compelled to coin a new phrase for it—extended action-meditation—discloses Lawrence's most elaborate nonfictional foray into an idealized polity. It also reveals an esthetic integral to this societal vision and to a substantial portion of Lawrence's writings, as well as a kind of subjectivistic thinking that sensitively interprets the distant past.

A major underpinning in *Etruscan Places* is the contrasting of Etruria with an authoritarian, mechanized society (Rome, or "Rome"). Realization of the physical sensuous self by an entire (but caste-structured) society embodies the immortality here, a paradoxical effect rendered all the more subtle and poignant by Lawrence's pronounced distaste in this book for all forms of permanence. In *Apocalypse*, a work permeated with elitism, one encounters engaging signs of antiapocalyptic and antianthropomorphism. Rebirth now becomes the humanizing release incorporated in one's overcoming the need to deify or to indulge in the colossal retaliations basic to apocalyptic thinking.

One method employed in examining these two books is to establish a foil by which to test various qualities in Lawrence's interpretations. Etruscology and historiography highlight the strengths and weaknesses in *Etruscan Places*. Lawrence's book reveals in turn the limitations of an objectivist approach to Etruria (and, by extension, to professional interpretations of antiquity generally). A similar handling of Biblical scholarship and commentary will be found in the chapter on *Apocalypse*. Lawrence's iconoclastic and heterodoxical critique is set in relief through being contrasted with more traditional *Revelation* studies, as well as with the sharply opposed interpretations of such social theorists as Friedrich Engels and the millenialist scholar Norman Cohn. What becomes apparent in this inquiry is the profoundly human need—persisting from the cultures of the ancient Near East to the present—to project hope for an end to societal repression to the ultimate limits of the mythopoeic universe. Also evident are the cosmic, pathological fantasies and retributions in which, as Lawrence realized, such high-pressured orderings of experience could culminate.

The chapter on Lawrence's last verse, *Last Poems*, like that on *The Virgin and the Gipsy*, offers literary criticism. I have attempted to locate in this collection figures of centripetality and centrifugality that suggest respectively involuted life-denial and liberating life-affirmation. The death-rebirth patterns in this essay, as in some of the other chapters, suggest both a negative death or death-in-life on the one hand, and a literal and/or figurative death on the other connoting rebirth as fulfillment of being.

Death-and-rebirth analysis is not a new way of looking at Lawrence. A concept, an awareness so pivotal to Lawrence's vitalist thinking and feeling about human existence, is bound to have been discussed before. But this conception has not been utilized in any critical studies to probe all the superior writings of the last years. It offers both flexibility of meaning as a critical tool and accessibility to other disciplines besides English studies.

In this last body of work, along with memorable art and thought, lies a stunning evocation of man at the center and extremity of being. Lawrence, who felt compelled to say so much about how to live, also had something to say about the "deaths of man." Ultimately, the two concerns are one. What Lawrence said about the "deaths" he uttered with a tranquility, depth, and attractiveness that should endow these final works of creative thanatology and renewal with abiding stature. Thanks to Lawrence, his readers can perhaps address themselves to the lesser deaths of daily experience and to the ultimate one with reduced terror, more understanding, and no little excitement.

Notes

1. Aldous Huxley, ed., "Introduction" to *The Letters of D. H. Lawrence* (New York: Viking Press, 1932), p. 30.

Introduction

2. George H. Ford, *Double Measure: a Study of the Novels and Stories of D. H. Lawrence* (New York: Holt, Rinehart, & Winston, 1965), p. 97.

3. Ford, p. 97. See also Harry T. Moore, *The Priest of Love: A Life of D. H. Lawrence* (New York: Farrar, Straus, & Giroux, 1974), p. 42. Mark Spilka has observed that Fr. William Tiverton perceives a crucial death-rebirth event in the *Sons and Lovers* phase from another perspective: "Paul's death as a son implies his birth as a man and the potential birth of Lawrence himself as man and artist." *The Love Ethic of D. H. Lawrence* (Bloomington, Ind.: Indiana University Press, 1955), p. 39.

4. Stephen Spender, "D. H. Lawrence, England, and the War," in *D. H. Lawrence: Novelist, Poet, and Prophet* (New York: Harper & Row, 1973) states that "Not only was England killed for him [Lawrence], but there was also a sense in which the war killed him. For he was a man who died several deaths before he died" (p. 72).

5. Cf. Roger Sale's view *Modern Heroism: Essays on D. H. Lawrence, William Empson, and J. R. R. Tolkien* (Berkeley, Calif.: University of California Press, 1973) ". . . imaginatively he [Lawrence] could only repeat himself in the last fourteen years of his life" (p. 106).

6. Moore, *The Priest of Love,* p. 400.

7. L. D. Clark, *Dark Night of the Body: D. H. Lawrence's The Plumed Serpent* (Austin, Tex.: University of Texas Press, 1964), p. 49. See also Peter L. Irvine and Anne Kiley, eds., "D. H. Lawrence and Frieda Lawrence: Letters of Dorothy Brett," in *The D. H. Lawrence Review* Vol. 9. No. 1 (Spring 1976):16.

8. Examples of general studies positing a "last-period" Lawrence are: David Cavitch, *D. H. Lawrence and the New World* (1969); Graham Hough, *The Dark Sun: a Study of D. H. Lawrence* (1957); Frank Kermode, *D. H. Lawrence* (1973); Harry T. Moore, *The Priest of Love* (1974); R. E. Pritchard, *D. H. Lawrence, Body of Darkness* (1971); Keith Sagar, *The Art of D. H. Lawrence* (1966); Mark Schorer, *D. H. Lawrence* (1968). A few examples of genre studies are Sandra M. Gilbert, *Acts of Attention: The Poems of D. H. Lawrence* (1972) and Tom Marshall, *The Psychic Mariner* (1971). William York Tindall's *The Later D. H. Lawrence* (1952) is a selective anthology of the last works, with an appreciative introduction ("His final period," says Tindall, "is one of comparative fulfillment"—p.v).

9. James C. Cowan, *D. H. Lawrence and the American Journey* (Cleveland, Ohio: Case Western Reserve Press, 1964), 136-37.

10. Ibid., pp. 136-37.

11. ibid., p. 137. I am indebted to both Cowan and Keith Sagar (*The Art of D. H. Lawrence*) on this key transitional fiction for my position in this study about a late-Lawrence period.

12. David Cavitch, *D. H. Lawrence and the New World* (New York: Oxford University press, 1969), p. 193.

13. Ibid., p. 190.

14. Exceptions to this situation are: Christopher Hassall, "D. H. Lawrence and the Etruscans," *Essays by Divers Hands* 31 (1962): 61-78; L. D. Clark, "The Apocalypse of Lorenzo," *The D. H. Lawrence Review* Vol. 3, No. 2 (Summer 1970): 141-60; Mary Doyle Springer, *Forms of the Modern Novella* (Chicago: University of Chicago Press, 1975), 142-48; M. G. Krishnamurti, *D. H. Lawrence: Tale as a Medium* (Mysore: Rao and Raghavan, 1970). The last two books contain respective-

ly a section and a chapter dealing with *The Virgin and the Gipsy.* Kingsley Widmer *(The Art of Perversity: D. H. Lawrence's Shorter Fictions* (Seattle, Wash.: University of Washington Press, 1962)) has pointed out the central presence of a rebirth theme in Lawrence's last works: "The rebirth motif dominates Lawrence's late work—as a trope in stories like *The Virgin and the Gipsy,* "Sun," and *Lady Chatterley's Lover;* as a subject for essays and verses; and as an unresolvable answer to Lawrence's old obsession with death and oblivion in several fictional fragments" (p. 201).

15. Edwin S. Shneidman, *Deaths of Man* (Baltimore, Md.: Penguin Books, 1974), p. 44.

2

Lapsing Out:
Ideas of Mortality and Immortality in Lawrence

I

Colin Clarke in *River of Dissolution: D. H. Lawrence and English Romanticism* has developed the thesis that the nineteenth-century English Romantic poets explored states of dissolution as a way of arriving at "strange modes of being." He states, further, that D. H. Lawrence, deeply influenced by this tradition, elaborates motifs of dissolution both positively and negatively and with considerable sophistication in such works as *Women in Love*. "Like the Romantics, Lawrence is endlessly concerned with what Keats has called 'self-destroying'—the process of dying into being, the lapsing of consciousness which is yet the discovery of a deeper consciousness, the dissolution of the hard, intact, ready-defined ego . . ." (p. 3). This chapter will discuss "dying into being" in such key works as *Women in Love*, *Sons and Lovers*, and *The Man Who Died* (as well as *Twilight in Italy* and *The Rainbow* briefly), ending with a scrutiny of an important late poem entitled "Shadows."

Lawrence was hardly the first person to concern himself with the ambiguity and numinosity surrounding human death. Dying into new life is of course a basic religious conception, the loss or discarding of the old self and the birth of a new one patently a concept and feeling universally experienced. Human beings have usually desired to evade death in one way or another, and Lawrence was undoubtedly influenced by the wealth of means provided by Biblical eschatology to make just such an evasion conceivable. But Lawrence's transvaluative orientation offers an original perspective to the idea of rebirth. If one was to be reborn, it was not to be in the spirit, as Christianity would have it, but in the flesh. As formulated by Lawrence in his late novella and parable *The Man Who Died*, the Resurrection would effect a phallic Christ ("Lo! I am risen!," says the Man-"Christ" in the temple of Isis, a line embodying a kind of comic immortality all its own). Thus the Lawrentian new life in one large respect is connected with love, particularly with sexual love, as is evident in *Sons and Lovers*, *The Rainbow*, *The Man Who Died*, and *Lady Chatterley's Lover*. "Sex is really only touch," says Lawrence in *Lady Chatterley's Lover*, "the closest of all touch. And it's touch we're afraid of. We're only half-conscious, and half-alive. We've got to come alive and aware."[2]

But, as this passage indicates, Lawrence seldom treats sexual love as an end in itself; in *Sons and Lovers* sex is a dramatized value contending with a high-pressurized home and work environment. As Frank Kermode has stated, "the prophetic fury is woven into the silk."[3] Elsewhere in Lawrence's work, sex functions synecdochically, serving as the outward manifestation of a spiritual quest or fulfillment. Sex here is the body *and* soul of men and women. Resurrection, the "spiritual" new life, occurs through a sexual agency—and transcends into the body. Norman O. Brown, locating this idea in Tertullian and in the French theologian Jean Danielou (while curiously ignoring its presence in Lawrence), gives it a stunning formulation in *Love's Body*:

> Platonic allegiances, and sublimation, ascend from 'sensibles' to 'spirituals': for Platonism, the invisible and incor-

poreal things that are in heaven are true, while the visible and corporeal things on earth are copies of the true things, not themselves true. Symbolical consciousness—Christian, or psychoanalytical, or Dionysian—terminates in the body, remains faithful to the earth. The dreamer awakes not from a body but to a body. Not an ascent from body to spirit, but the descent of spirit into body: incarnation not sublimation. Hence to find the true meaning of history is to find the bodily meaning.[4]

The new self-realization permeates *Women in Love*. It is evoked as theory within a dramatized context in the chapter entitled "School Lesson," when Birkin, berating the "dead" Hermione, presents a plan of resuscitation for Hermione and Ursula (and the reader):

'There's the whole difference in the world,' he said, 'between the actual sensual being and the vicious mental-deliberate profligacy *our* [italics added] lot goes in for. In our nighttime, there's always the electricity switched on, we watch ourselves, we get it all in the head, really. You've got to lapse out before you can know what sensual reality is, lapse into unknowingness, and give up your volition. You've got to do it. You've got to learn not-to-be, before you can come into being.'[5]

The irony here, and part of the tension in *Women in Love*, is that Birkin too is nearly dead (as my italics in the passage suggest), and must undergo a transformation to survive. Mark Schorer divides the characters into those who are (or will be) alive and those (such as Gerald, Gudrun, Hermione, and Loerke) who are "dead" or dying ("*fleurs du mal*," as Birkin calls them). The characters who lack the regenerative energy for a new life are not only figuratively but literally imperilled, as the case of Gerald Crich, representing a leader and apex of modern mechanized humanity, makes clear.

But even the "life" characters in *Women in Love* are at times engrossed with death. Near the end of "Water Party," a crucial chapter in orienting Gerald toward his own destruction, Birkin says to Ursula: "There is a life which belongs to death, and there is a life which isn't death. One is tired of the life that belongs to death—our kind of life. . . . I *do* want to die from this life. . . . One is delivered over like a naked infant from the womb . . . the old body gone, and new air around one, that has never been breathed before" (p. 178). This passage is clearly concerned with figurative death for Birkin, but in the succeeding chapter, "Sunday Evening," Ursula herself (with Lawrence certainly at her elbow, if not speaking through her lips) has death meditations of broader import:

"Death is a great consummation, a consummating experience. It is a development from life. That we know, while we are yet living. What then need we think for further? One can never see beyond the consummation. It is enough that death is a great and conclusive experience. Why should we ask what comes after the experience, when the experience is still unknown to us?" [P. 183]

'Does the body correspond so immediately with the spirit?' she asked herself. And she knew, with the clarity of ultimate knowledge, that the body is only one of the manifestations of the spirit, the transmutation of the integral spirit is the transmutation of the physical body as well. Unless I set my will, unless I absolve myself from the rhythm of life, fix myself and remain static, cut off from living, absolved within my own will. But better die than live mechanically a life that is a repetition of repetitions. To die is to move on with the invisible. To die is also a joy, a joy of submitting to that which is greater than the known; namely, the pure unknown.' [P.184]

The first quotation, almost as marked by groping as by assertiveness, should be regarded within an enveloping narrative framework. As such, it represents a stage for Ursula and "Birkin-Lawrence" in their progress from withdrawal from the "life" of the dominant society to the new life of their own evolving relationship. Both passages seem, in isolation, vague in their mysticism and affirmation. The second tempts

Ideas of Mortality and Immortality

one to the reductive reading that rebirth in this instance means that anything is more viable than modern industrialized societies. The "pure unknown" can mean anything, and thus nothing. But, dramatically, it serves as a "crisis-mysticism" for a primary character experiencing at this juncture of the narrative "the unutterable anguish of dissolution," before her new life with Birkin of "stars in conjunction" consolidated later in the novel. The outlook here is unambiguously grim enough, and vast and trenchant in its applicability: ". . . . where was life to be found? No flowers grow upon busy machinery, there is no sky to a routine, there is no space to a rotary motion, mechanized, cut off from reality. There was nothing to look for from life—it was the same in all countries and all peoples. The only window was death . . . one knew that the soul was a prisoner within this sordid vast edifice of life, and there was no escape, save in death" (p. 185).

Ultimately then, *Women in Love* depicts the "life" of society itself as being at stake. Even that of its hero and heroine hangs in the balance. Lawrence said in his 1919 Foreward to *Women in Love*, "We are now in a period of crisis. Every man who is acutely alive is acutely wrestling with his own soul." Those who can "lapse out" will survive. Those, like Hermione and Gerald, who cannot, not only will be destroyed, but will first destroy others as well (as Hermione very nearly destroys Birkin and Gerald Gudrun). Gerald, likened by Gudrun, another who can't lapse out and one of Gerald's destroyers, to Bismarck at one point, has already "deadened" many thousands of Midlands workers by his mechanistic perfecting of his father's coal mining industry; he incorporates the deadliness associated in *Women in Love* with characters strongly oriented toward "mental-deliberate profligacy" or will. The need for regenerative human beings, individuals "acutely alive," signifies a crucial countervailing motif to all the destroyers in Lawrence's most pronounced doomsday novel.

One mode of regeneracy appears early in Lawrence's

tuality. "Blood consciousness" (that unhappy phrase) stresses consciousness as well as "blood" to achieve that transcendent "supreme ecstasy."

Nature provides another important frame for Lawrence's treatment of ideas about death and resurrection. This usage appears memorably in the famous "peewits" sequence in *Sons and Lovers*:

> All the while [that Paul and Clara are making love] the peewits were screaming in the field. When he came to, he wondered what was near his eyes, curving and strong with life in the dark, and what voice it was speaking. Then he realised it was the grass, and the peewit was calling. The warmth was Clara's breathing heaving. He lifted his head, and looked into her eyes. They were dark and shining and strange, life wild at the source staring into his life, stranger to him, yet meeting him; and he put his face down on her throat, afraid. What was she? A strong, strange, wild life, that breathed with his in the darkness through this hour. It was all so much bigger than themselves that he was hushed. They had met, and included in their meeting the thrust of the manifold grass stems, the cry of the peewit, the wheel of the stars. . . .
>
> And after such an evening they both were very still, having known the immensity of passion. They felt small, half-afraid, childish and wondering, like Adam and Eve when they lost their innocence and realised the magnificence of the power which drove them out of Paradise and across the great night and the great day of humanity. It was for each of them an initiation and a satisfaction. To know their own nothingness, to know the tremendous living flood which carried them always, gave them rest within themselves. If so great a magnificent power could overwhelm them, identify them altogether with itself, so that they knew they were only grains in the tremendous heave that lifted every grass blade its little height, and every tree, and living thing, then why fret about themselves?

Both Paul and Clara will go on fretting about themselves. Yet for those readers who feel that Paul will survive the life-or-death crisis of his mother's death, this should be a key passage. Rather than using the passage to deal with that issue, however, I want to relate it to the idea of death and resurrection under scrutiny. What dies in this passage from *Sons and Lovers* is innocence in the form of Paul's ignorance of human connection with and thus validation by the living universe. The Garden of Eden allusion suggests a loss of a narrow sense of self on a religious and an archetypal level; it is a loss seen as desirable by the narrator himself. The "initation" (also described as a satisfaction) concerns Paul's new awareness through sexual love of his and Clara's incarnation of the grass, the peewits, the stars. Thus the experience also serves as a metaphoric means of indicating *through nature* their new consciousness of recesses of being in themselves surpassing the ego. "Why fret about themselves" in "the tremendous living flood which carried them *always* . . ." [my italics--D.G.]. Aside from the dramatic context in the narrative, the passage is transvaluative in depicting the expulsion as a good thing, offering Paul, furthermore, potential release from his emotional bondage to his parents. It also formulates a creed. The creed in some respects is similar to the one implicit in Birkin's exasperated advice to the tight-willed Hermione to die in the ego and come alive in some deeper way. The awesome finality and immobility of death is challenged here (and even more so in the novel's controversial concluding paragraph) by a vitalist ethic embodied as an imagery of movement or an ongoing process of nature ("the thrust of the manifold grass stems, the cry of the peewit, the wheel of the stars"). One might also allude to the rainbow arching over and ending *The Rainbow*, Lawrence's apocalyptic nature image of hope for renewal of Western man in the death-vise of industrialization.

That Lawrence could write well about literal death and dying is exemplified in several sections of *Sons and lovers* (not to mention important passages in *Women in Love* and the short stories). The death of Tom Brangwen in *The Rainbow* reveals violent death in that objective-subjective characterization that Lawrence could wield so effectively. Brangwen has come drunk from a tavern late at night and is confronted by a flood caused by a break in the canal adjacent to his farm:

> He went to meet the running flood, sinking deeper and deeper. His soul was full of great astonishment. He *had* to go and look where it came from, though the ground was going from under his feet. He went on, down towards the pond, shakily. He rather enjoyed it. He was knee-deep, and the water was pulling heavily. He stumbled, reeled sickeningly.
> Fear took hold of him. Gripping tightly to the lamp, he reeled, and looked around. The water was carrying his feet away, he was dizzy. He did not know which way to turn. The water was whirling, whirling, the whole black night was swooping in rings. He swayed uncertainly at the centre of all the attack, reeling in dismay. In his soul, he knew he would fall.
> As he staggered, something in the water struck his legs, and he fell. Instantly he was in the turmoil of suffocation, fighting, wrestling, but always borne down, borne inevitably down. Still he wrestled and fought to get himself free, in the unutterable struggle of suffocation, but he always fell again deeper. Something struck his head, a great wonder of anguish went over him, then the blackness covered him entirely.[8]

Lawrence is not always appreciated for his fictional realization of concrete or fundamental experiences, yet one would have to look far before finding in literature a description of a drowning more terrifying and empathetic than this. Further evidence of Lawrence's mastery in depicting violent biological death can be found shortly after in a description of Brangwen's corpse and in Anna Brangwen's response to the sight of her father's drowned body: "It was when they brought him to her house dead and in his wet clothes, his wet sodden clothes, fully dressed as he came from the market, yet all sodden and inert, that the shock really broke into her, and she was terrified. A big, soaked, inert heap he was, who had been to her the image of power and strong life" (p. 247). The motif of life's purposes (Brangwen dressed, going to market, the memory of his vital being) in sharp opposition to the details of death and its abruptness (the *wet* clothes, the "sodden and inert" body, an "inert heap") shock the reader as well as Anna. The credentials for portraying imaginative rebirth become all the more valid in being presented by an author who could record literal death so sensitively and unflinchingly.

II

In the last period of Lawrence's career, his treatment of mortality is exercised in some works within a more traditional mythic context than earlier. Seizing upon the definitive death-and-rebirth event in Western Christian civilization, Lawrence transforms it into his own mythos:

> Risen from the dead, he had realised at last that his body, too, has its little life and beyond that, the greater life. He was virgin, in recoil from the little, greedy life of the body. But now he knew that virginity is a form of greed; and that the body rises again to give and to take, to take and to give, ungreedily. Now he knew that he had risen from the woman, or women, who knew the greater life of the body, not greedy to take, not greedy to give, and with whom he could mingle his body. But having died, he was patient, knowing there was time, an eternity of time. And he was driven with no greedy desire, either to give himself to others, or to grasp anything for himself. For he had died.[9]

". . .the body rises again to give and to take, to take and to give, ungreedily." One thinks of Norman O. Brown's "The dreamer awakes not from a body but to a body." Lawrence's is an archetypal godly man. Brown's ideal maker and Lawrence's man-god or God-in-man share the "divinity" of realized corporeal being, "incarnation not sublimation," says Brown (and his two Christian authorities). If, quoting Brown once more, "to find the true meaning of history is to find the bodily meaning," then Heaven, Utopia, the New Jerusalem, the Classless Society, the Beloved Community, all the expressions for the dream of a humanely expressive and joyful society in one sense consummate in the body. They also can begin there. Yet if the meaning of history leads to the meaning of the body, and if the fate of the body is its termination, then history would seem to lead to its own destruction.

Indeed physical experience has traditionally been rejected as an authoritative sanction of value, a consideration often held against Lawrence. But the corporeal immortality both Brown and Lawrence are thinking of is the enhancement of life that derives from the full acceptance of the body. To fully accept the body is also to accept its end, to accept death. Brown has formulated the idea in *Life Against Death*, adding a historical perspective in a concluding chapter unsurprisingly titled "The Resurrection of the Body": "The death instinct is reconciled with the life instinct only in a life which is not repressed, which leaves no 'unlived lines' in the human body, the death instinct then being affirmed in a body which is willing to die. And, because the body is satisfied, the death instinct no longer drives it to change itself and make history, and therefore, as Christian theology divined, its activity is in eternity"[10]

Lawrence in a late essay called "The Risen Lord" again poses the idea of bodily immortality iconoclastically in Christian terms:

> ...Resurrection is indeed the consummation of all the passion. Not even atonement, the being at one with Christ through partaking in His sacrifice, consummates the Passion finally. For even after Atonement men still must live, and must go forward with the vision. After we share in the body of Christ, we rise with Him in the body. And that is the final vision that has been blurred to all the Churches.
> Christ risen in the flesh! We must accept the image complete, if we accept it at all. We must take the mystery in its fulness and in fact. It is only the image of our own experience. Christ rises, when He rises from the dead, in the flesh, not merely as spirit. He rises with hands and feet, as

Thomas knew for certain: and if with hands and feet, then with lips and stomach and genitals of a man. Christ risen, and risen in the whole of His flesh, not with some left out.[11]

These ideas of bodily immortality are not only the "Death-where-is-thy-sting?" declamation of the stout soul who has mastered the natural fear of death. Nor do they represent glibly optimistic formulations of figurative death. Brown and Lawrence are positing the existence of an unknown region in our physical being that has been buried or denigrated by powerful conservative traditions of moral censorship and spiritual authority. If the thesis of the greater reality of a corporeal to a spiritual eschatology begs the question about the word "reality," one can point to the mystical basis of this heterodoxical position, and, as such, the authority of its truth residing in the individual.

Strictures of Lawrence's body-mysticism often ignore its integral position in the more complex patterns in his art. A major polarity of concept and motif in his work is the apocalyptic mode on the one hand, and the presentation of the here-and-now nature of human experience on the other. Implied in this latter category, besides the conventional notion of mortality, is both the immortality of the fully seized moment, and also, paradoxically and satisfyingly, its mortality. This aspect of "momentaneity" and "realization" emerges frequently and variedly in Lawrence, as in "Why the Novel Matters" when he states: "Paradise is *after* life, and I for one am not keen on anything that is *after* life."[12] But the apocalyptic vision, in which new life follows a death-inclined period of violence and decadence, offers the millennial immortality of a future Happy Age, and thus creates a subtle interaction with Lawrence's powerfully conveyed here-and-now motifs. The combination of these two antithetical modes of representing human experience lends all the "structure" and "texture" and "irony" one could want to Lawrence's better work. Certainly these modes usually inform his best art.

What can also be "immortal" in human physical finitude,

Ideas of Mortality and Immortality 39

present both in Lawrence's metaphysics of sex and in his libertarian aspect, is the right of every human being to grow and develop free of domination (whether familial or institutional). This affirmation is mythically sexual in *The Man Who Died*. But its larger implications operate through the vastly general and generic religious sense that Lawrence attempts to secure by calling Christ "the Man." Though there is something of himself in this character (as there obviously was in some of his paintings), he also intends his character to retain some of the traditional aura of sacred significance. This religious authority of Lawrence's personnage, defined sexually in a death-and-rebirth context, is perhaps Lawrence's most audacious gesture in handling a rebirth theme; he attempts to bolster it by introducing a mystical conception that figures both in this novella as well as in "The Flying Fish": "He had come back to life, but not the same life that he had left, the life of the little people and the little day. Re-born, he was in the other life, the greater day of the human consciousness"[13]

What does the idea of the greater day of the "human consciousness" signify? In part it is "the greater life of the body, beyond the little, nervous, personal life" (p. 178). This definition acquires a "pagan" mythic significance through the Man, readily identifiable with Christ, also presenting himself as Osiris to the priestess of Isis. Lawrence is perhaps having his mythical cake and eating it too, by invoking for his "Man" both the apocalypticism of Christian and Joachite messianism and the "pagan" cycle realism of the Mediterranean vegetation-fertility gods. The "little life," an alternate expression Lawrence uses for the "lesser day," is also "giving without taking" (p. 179), and, as one form of the ethic of self-denial, another repudiation of the traditional Christ, and thus of Christian immortality.

One more aspect of the "greater day" and the "greater life" is the "immortality" enjoyed by "the Man" after he survives crucifixion to become "alive without fret. . . . Now his uncaring self healed and became whole within his skin, and he smiled to himself with pure aloneness, which is one sort of immortality" (p. 180). Destructive, ultimately genocidal, mortality is described shortly after by the narrator as "the mania of cities and societies and hosts, to lay a compulsion upon a man, upon all men. For men and women alike were made with the egotistic fear of their own nothingness. And he thought of his own mission, how he had tried to lay the compulsion of love on all men" (p. 184).

We are back to Lawrence's grand theme of domination, the perversion of instinct *and* mind in order to control and inevitably dehumanize the sensibilities of other human beings. Sons, lovers, daughters, spouses, in earlier works, and now, in *The Man Who Died*, mankind itself and its fundamental ethical institutions are exposed to the radical charge of compulsion by Lawrence's own "compulsion" of the pivotal personnage of Western Christendom. Surely a more revolutionary rendering of "subject matter" would be difficult to imagine. Nor is it surprising that Lawrence's next large effort at fiction was at first entitled *Tenderness*, for tenderness would seem more likely to issue from living "without fret" and with "insouciance" (a favorite word of his at this time)[14] than from the urge to dominate.

Considering the proximity to his last period of the three leadership novels, Lawrence's conceptions of immortality during the late twenties suggest a transcendence of the "mortality" of his own willfulness and domineering. Yet this is not entirely so, for a sharp class discrimination can be identified even in this symbolic fable. More than once in *The Man Who Died*, those in the "lesser day," the routine life of everyday concerns, are seen as lower-class. They are the "little people," the peasants, farmers, "commoners" of a society: "Why then should [they] be lifted up? Clods of earth . . . are not to be lifted up" (p. 172). Later we are told this about slaves spreading fishing nets on a beach: "All-tolerant Pan should be their god forever" (p. 197). The bodily egalitarianism in his literary art even during this late period would not totally eradicate Lawrence's rooted class snobbery, evident even in his last book, *Apocalypse*. It also appears in *Lady Chatterley's Lover* with Mellors' approval: " 'the few [Mellors includes himself] can go in for the higher cults if they like. . . . But let the mass be forever pagan' "[15] Lawrence, here and in some of the other last period writings, becomes identifiable with Dostoevski's Grand Inquisitor and the authoritarian mystique of Miracle, Mystery, and Authority. But the sensitivity, variety, and force of his conceptions of immortality during this period assuage the unattractiveness of his views on class. For, embedded within the class hierarchies in some of Lawrence's writings, lies a profound realization that partly humanizes them: "Unless we encompass it [the lesser day, the lesser life] in the greater day, and set the little life in the circle of the greater life, all is disaster" (p. 200).

Being reborn through a Lawrentian agency, however, the Man will not set out again to change the world, but to realize his own self. Since the Man will return in the Spring like Osiris, rather than ascend like Christ, the mode of immortality operating in the story is clearly the pre-Christian, seasonal, cyclic one that Lawrence saw all around him in the Florence countryside during the twenties as he was slowly dying. The implication obtains that great, even god-like men (like Lawrence's "Christ" and "Osiris") will recur as inevitably as the seasons to embody "Holy Living" and "Holy Dying" for humanity.

III

Near the end of his life, Lawrence wrote a long essay called "Introduction to His Paintings." An ideological preface to his exhibition of paintings at the Warren Gallery in London, it traces the psychological impact of syphilis on European painting from the Renaissance to the twentieth century. In the process the essay also offers a mythic formulation of the annihilation of body-acceptance in the mind of European man and thus in the visual arts as well. It posits both the nature of this "death" and the terms of rebirth in a characteristic manner:

> The terror-horror element struck a blow at our feeling of physical communion. In fact, it almost killed it. We have become ideal beings, creatures that exist in idea, to one another, rather than flesh-and-blood kin. And with the collapse of the feeling of physical, flesh-and-blood kinship, and the substitution of our ideal, social or political oneness, came the failing of our intuitive awareness, and the great unease, the *nervousness* of mankind. We are *afraid* of the intuition within us. We suppress the instincts, and we cut off our intuitional awareness from one another and the world. The reason being some great shock to the procreative self.... Intuitively we are dead to one another, we have all gone cold.[16]

The argument climaxes a few pages later again in a figurative declamation of "life" and "death" applicable to everyone: "At the maximum of our imagination we are religious. And if we deny our imagination, and have no imaginative life, we are poor worms who have never lived" (p. 317). The realization of the imagination is in turn dependent upon an acceptance of imagery that he denotes as "the body of our imaginative life." The radical fear of syphilis, Lawrence claims, has alienated us from the body, and killed our imaginative faculties. The modern result is a psyche that he describes in the essay "Pornography and Obscenity," again in symbolically sexual terms, as "a vicious circle of self-enclosure, masturbating self-consciousness...." In "A Propos of *Lady Chatterley's Lover*," he judges this condition as a deathly "white" sex which is distinguished from "red" sex: "... nearly all modern sex is a pure matter of nerves, cold and bloodless.... But whereas the contact in the urge of blood-desire is positive, making a newness in the blood, in the insistence of this nervous, personal desire, the blood-contact becomes frictional and destructive ..."[18]

This psycho-sexual maiming, Lawrence contends, has

destroyed the universe for us. We are like "a great uprooted tree, with its roots in the air. We must plant ourselves again in the universe"(p. 354). This sense of a lost cosmos and cosmic awareness Lawrence elaborates in *Apocalypse* (which we will consider at length in Chapter 6).

Lawrence's versatile handling of death-and-rebirth elements may be observed from still another perspective by comparing the early poem "Love on the Farm" with a few major poems from his *Last Poems*. Among other things, this comparison displays a figurative death as love in the early piece, and a literal, biological death in the latter. Yet the difference is not so much one of subject, sex, and love in the early or earlier writings, and a mystical, nonsexual identification with nature in the late verse. Furthermore, the subject of nature, as well as the presence of symbolic light and dark imagery, is found throughout the Lawrence canon. The difference between a poem like "Love on the Farm" and two late poems such as "The Ship of Death" and "Shadows" is tonal; in the latter poems, Lawrence, by exerting his whole being toward a mystical understanding and acceptance of death, effects a serenity that in artistic terms can be expressed as a sustained dramatic sovereignty over his creative warring selves in any number of Lawrentian formulations: the "daimon" and the "young man," mind (or soul) and body, light versus dark, subject and object, self and the other (or the world), and so on.

Both "Love on the Farm" and the two poems from *Last Poems* are clearly poems about mortality and immortality, yet the authority of consummately "felt experience" and the resultant serenity, so integral to the greatness of the late poems, are missing in the early poem. What "Love on the Farm" possesses instead is a tone of nearly uncontrolled hysteria and a pervasive primitivist violence or menace that seems *gauche* compared to "The Ship of Death." Compared, however, to representative and coeval Georgian poems ("What is this life, if, full of care, / We have no time to stand

and stare. / No time to stand beneath the boughs / And stare as long as sheep or cows",[19] "Love on the Farm" evinces originality and a startling dramatized primitivity. In this poem the whole rural universe, flora and fauna as well as humanity, is alive with fear of man as death-bringer-and lover. Nature, the sedate prop of the English Romantic poets, here quivers into sentience: the "evening's anxious breast," "the woodbine . . . calling low to her lover," the swallow and "her marriage bed," the terror of the swallow and the water hen as the farmer-lover strides by, and the fear of the rabbit, pressing back "her" ears, "with wild spring" spurting "from the terror of his oncoming" (and rightly so, as the rabbit is soon throttled by the man), all of the terror viewed through the female "I" narrator of the poem, who sees it all, furthermore, as a prelude to her own death:

He flings the rabbit soft on the table board
And comes toward me: ah! the uplifted sword
Of his hand against my bosom, and oh, the broad
Blade of his glance that asks me to applaud
His coming! With his hand he turns my face to him
And caresses me with his fingers that still smell grim
Of rabbit's fur! God, I am caught in a snare!
I know not what fine wire is round my throat;
I only know I let him finger there
My pulse of life, and let him nose like a stoat
Who sniffs with joy before he drinks the blood.

And down his mouth comes to my mouth! and down
His bright dark eyes come over me, like a hood
Upon my mind! his lips meet mine, and a flood
Of sweet fire sweeps across me, so I drown
Against him, die, and find death good.[20]

The imagery of imminent violence in this passage ("uplifted sword of his hand," "blade of his glance") combined with the narrator's self-victimizing double association with the slaughtered rabbit (menaced by both man and ferret) moves the poem toward its culmination in death. But the reader is

Ideas of Mortality and Immortality

presented with the "little death" of sexual self-transcendence rather than with the literal mortality of *Last Poems* verse. Mixing his metaphors with an audacity reminiscent of the Metaphysical poets ("flood of sweet fire"), the speaker in the poem "dies," and says it is a "good death." Presumably she is reborn to a more stable psychoemotional existence, the world of living things still vibrant for her, though less prone perhaps to be inducted into another hysterical drama, exactly because of that "good death," and of its authority as a refining and stabilizing experience in the inner life. Yet the entire poem is so deeply submerged in extreme feelings associating death with love, that, despite the happy outcome, the element of death is not to be lightly dismissed. For even if it intimates the melodramatized psyche of an overwrought young woman (and young poet), it also is evidence of a characteristic mode of Lawrence's creative imagination appearing throughout his work.

In the late poems, nature itself is so rendered as to provide examples of and a medium for both mortality and immortality, as "The Ship of Death" indicates:

Now it is autumn and the falling fruit
and the long journey towards oblivion

The apples falling like great drops of dew
to bruise themselves an exit from themselves

And it is time to go, to bid farewell
to one's own self, and find an exit
from the fallen self.[21]

The dying man in the poem "lapses out" toward death and "death" as oblivion, or "nowhere," the ineluctable prerequisite for rebirth:

There is no port, there is nowhere to go
only the deepening blackness darkening still
blacker upon the soundless, ungurgling flood

darkness at one with darkness, up and down
and sideways utterly dark, so there is no direction any more.
and the little ship is there; yet she is gone.
She is not seen, for there is nothing to see her by.
She is gone! gone! and yet
somewhere she is there.
Nowhere!

After this total obliteration of one's human existence and/or
of one's carapace-like ego, the new self emerges:

The flood subsides, and the body, like a worn seashell
emerges strange and lovely.
And the little ship wings home, faltering and lapsing
on the pink flood,
and the frail soul steps out, into her house again
filling the heart with peace.

Swings the heart renewed with peace
even of oblivion.

IV

"The Ship of Death" is one of Lawrence's best poems, yet "Shadows," a relatively unknown poem, has its own integrity and uniqueness as a poetic testament on mortality and immortality. As such, it deserves more attention than it has received to date.

"Shadows" is one (and one of the best) of the "oblivion" poems from Lawrence's *Last Poems*. Some of the other oblivion poems are "Bavarian Gentians" (in a special sense) and the poem preceding "Shadows" in the Pinto-Roberts *Complete Poems of D. H. Lawrence* entitled "Temples":

Oh, what we want on earth
is centres here and there of silence and forgetting

Ideas of Mortality and Immortality 47

where we may cease from knowing, and, as far as we know,
may cease from being
in the sweet wholeness of oblivion.²²

This poem, like many of the poems in *Last Poems*, proffers a modern mode of holy dying in which dying and death are regarded as experiences revealing humanity's affinity with nature. "Bavarian Gentians" depicts this affinity on the plane of myth. Pluto and Persephone "royally" incarnate and thus ennoble death and sex, and, by extension, man, who beholds these prime events as august mysteries. But, "Bavarian Gentians" also marks the beginning of the crucial strain in *Last Poems* of the ambiguous death by presenting death in metaphors of sexuality and immortality that simultaneously suggest regeneration. If "The Ship of Death" images the experience of dying less romantically than "Bavarian Gentians," it also conceives death in the concluding two stanzas as accessible to some kind of figurative rebirth. However, such poems as "Difficult Death" (which follows "The Ship of Death") and "Change" insist that even a religious acceptance of death will not make it easy to accept, and that "oblivion" can be austere and "bitter":

It is not easy to die, O it is not easy
to die the death

For death comes when he will
not when we will him.²³

Yet there is perhaps hope:

Maybe life is still our portion
after the bitter passage of oblivion.

"Difficult Death" is a slight poem, but a necessary link to "Shadows," which is situated two poems from the end of *The Complete Poems*, and thus was probably written by Lawrence very near the end of his life. The poem can stand by itself, unlike some of the other short "link" poems such as "Know-All," "Sleep," or "Forget," which are apothegms on the subject of oblivion, brief ejaculations between poems such as "The Ship of Death" and "Shadows" designed to establish a varying rhythm of concern with the larger meditative poems. In "Shadows," however, the thematic concerns of many of the oblivion poems culminate in an equilibrium quite different from the ritualization of dying and the exaltation of life-after-death found in "The Ship of Death." "Shadows" is a deeply personalized poem (that is not to say it is a poem of merely personal experience). The persona of the poem is clearly, though not exclusively, the dying Lawrence. But what is so striking in "Shadows" is the extraordinary serenity embodied in its movement toward a vision of God, which, in Lawrence's fidelity to his own ideas, is an "unknown" God. Even at the end, the "dark gods" are still there.

A dialectic can be recognized in the poem as a thesis of the drift toward death—"my spirit darkens and goes out, and soft strange gloom / pervades my movements and my thoughts and words"[24] which moves immediately into a paradoxical antithesis—"then I shall know that I am walking still / with God, we are close together now the moon is in shadow" (11.8-9). The third and largest stanza of the poem has the same dialectical progression (as does the fourth stanza) from a movement toward death back to the sense of continuing life:

And if as autumn deepens and darkens
I feel the pain of falling leaves, and stems that break in storms
and trouble and dissolution and distress
and then the softness of deep shadows folding, folding
around my soul and spirit . . .

moving again a few lines later into its antithetical affirmative phases:

Then I shall know that my life is moving still
with the dark earth, and drenched
with the deep oblivion of earth's lapse and renewal.

The final stanza of the poem, stanza six, operates as a synthesis because of its position in the poem and because it broaches a revelation that runs counter to the death-oriented sentiments in the poem. But stanza six is synthesizing for the more important reason that it possesses a concentrated eschatological force asserting the certainty of personal resurrection *because* of the preceding evidence of thesis and antithesis:

Then[italics added] I must know that still
I am in the hands [of] the unknown God.
he is breaking me down to his own oblivion
to send me forth on a new morning, a new man.

The schema of life-death-new life embodies the shape of meanings in the poem because it stresses phases, and phases in this area of experience depend, according to Lawrence, on a choice made with the whole of one's last being. The choice in the poem is a familiar enough paradox; the "new life," the personal resurrection, will not be achieved unless one accepts death. The promises of a new life through the acceptance of death involves, however, an extreme act of faith, for what must be accepted is the obliteration of the egoistic core of one's own consciousness. This most trying of self-abnegations is a central theme in Lawrence's *Last Poems*. In "Shadows," however, the process of dying seems on first glance to be depicted in a manner that renders the human being and nature identical. In "The Ship of Death," the relation between humanity and nature ("falling fruit" and apples) is viewed analogically, as a similitude. The dying of nature and of man in part I of "The Ship of Death" is seen as an experience held in common but also encountered separately.

In "Shadows" the process of similitude also occurs, as when the ailing narrator speaks of waking "like a new-opened flower." But nature in this poem is frequently not even distanced by similitude; it penetrates the dying man through Lawrence's empathy:

> . . . in the dark of the moon
> my spirit darkens and goes out (St. 2)
> I feel the pain of falling leaves, and
> stems that break in storms . . . (St. 3)
> and then the softness of deep shadows folding, folding
> around my soul and spirit, around my lips (St. 3)
> then I shall know that my life is moving still
> with the dark earth, and drenched
> with the deep oblivion of earth's lapse and
> renewal. (St. 3)

Yet part of the pathos and irony of "Shadows" derives from the fact that humanity and nature are not identical on any level. Lawrence is thus wedging the acceptance of man's ideal unity with nature against the Wordsworthian lament that adulthood severs one from any comforting organic context. This countervailing is not obtrusive, but then "Shadows" is not a strident poem. Where, then, does one find evidence of this separation? The conditional clause structure implies it: "And *if* tonight . . ." the speaker finds peace in sleep; he may not. Furthermore, he may not wake "like a new-opened flower" in the morning; he may not wake at all. This anxious doubt indeed forms part of the wish to propitiate the "shadows" through an attempt at a Romanticist merging with them; the title image of the poem, despite the Lawrentian ethic of a "good" darkness, carries the traditional association of mortal terror. Union with nature, then, is not entirely comforting, for it coerces identification with the seasonal decline, and offers the grim inevitability of feeling one's life "moving still with the dark earth."

This low-keyed conflict of doubt and faith, of fear and assurance, is also paradoxically resolved in the last three lines of the third stanza ("then I shall know that my life is moving still / with the dark earth, and drenched / with the deep oblivion of earth's lapse and renewal"), and in the fifth stanza ("odd wintry flowers upon the withered stem, yet new, strange flowers / such as my life has not brought forth before, new blossoms of me"). In this stanza Lawrence's assimilation

Ideas of Mortality and Immortality

of nature operates metaphorically twice. The dying man, lying in bed, vulnerable to the sensations of ebbing strength and misery, "flowers" both "wintry" and "new" flowers. "Wintry" (or old) and "new" because man as both a physical and religious being has two lives, the departing life of the body, and the renascence in humanity's participation in the life of nature. Not only is there an identification with other organic life, but dying itself offers something strangely new: "new blossoms of me." The paradoxical rendering of human mortality as immortality through an identification with nature is amplified by the covert metaphor in the same stanza of "flowers" on "withered stem" in which we can discern a figure of the human body and sensibility conceived as a flowering plant or tree.

"Shadows" offers a thesis and antithesis of life and death, rising into a synthesis of new life through Lawrence's nature-mysticism. But the poem operates more subtly than this discursive and schematic approach indicates. It functions through the "poetic" paradox of perceiving and projecting an ultimate unity of purpose in life and death. As I have tried to show, it is not difficult to support this notion through Lawrence's own tradition of manipulating darkness transvaluatively to affirm life and regeneration. One thinks of the "dark gods," that chthonian pantheon of unconscious energies, which, evoked and properly assimilated, offer the new "life" of revelation and an enhanced integrity of being. And certainly one can locate a diction of creative, affirmative darkness in the poem, starting with "oblivion" in line two, "dark earth" and "deep oblivion" in stanza three, "lovely oblivion" and, culminatingly, "his [the unknown God's] own oblivion," in stanzas five and six. Yet this strategy is not the central one in Lawrence's dramatized progression of the fear man—and particularly a dying man—has of his separateness from everything to a serenity arising from his faith in human participation in the immortality of nature.

Searching for the basic perspective on death and rebirth in

the poem leads one back to Colin Clarke's thesis of dissolution. Applied to "Shadows," "creative dissolution" functions as a pivotal action by which the translation from dying to a hope of new life is established. It centers on the word "swoon" in the sixth line of the third stanza, that pinpoints the dissolution essential to experiencing a new state of mind. The swoon describes the sensation—"so sweet"—that the Lawrence persona has of "soft" deep shadows "folding/ around my soul and spirit" and (significantly including the body) "around my lips." The word is also likened to a "drowse," another synonym for lapsing consciousness. Both "swoon" and "drowse" are used to describe the "deep shadows" that the persona is encountering. The "shadows" are like a song, like in effect the song of Keats's nightingale, only "darker." Clarke asserts that Keats's "Ode to a Nightingale" is the *locus classicus* of Romanticist dissolution. Certainly the "Ode" looms behind "Shadows" and this stanza in particular. But the acute poignancy and deliberate metaphysical irresolution of Keats's poem contrast with the cyclic affirmative movement in "Shadows" toward a hard-earned serenity. Lawrence's "shadows" intimate not only the death preceding another life; they betoken a real mortality for both season or nature and humanity. Keats "dissolves" temporarily into a vision of art and nature as immortality, then "recomposes" back into a present so imbued with a sense of life's misery as to be a death-in-life. Lawrence is swooning into a death that is a real death but also, as projected by the entire poem, by many poems in *Last Poems*, and by the works in the Lawrence canon already considered, the symbolic and mystic death without which no rebirth is possible.

"Shadows" lacks the tragic depth of Keats's "Ode," yet it possesses qualities rare in any age and almost nonexistent in ours. Few modern works of art attempt to make us face death tranquilly. "Shadows" is permeated with serenity, not in the stark, ritualized manner of "The Ship of Death," nor with the erotic grandeur of "Bavarian Gentians," but with a courageous warmth of confident personal utterance in the last extremity. "Shadows" is a brave poem; although it posits a (not necessarily human) restoration, death is not diminished. Lawrence pays homage to the darkest of the dark gods, the "unknown God," and, in fully submitting to his own hermetics of psychic and physical decomposition, gains the immortality of a consummated artistic integrity.

Notes

1. Colin Clarke, *River of Dissolution: D. H. Lawrence and English Romanticism* (New York: Barnes & Noble, 1969), p.3. Further references to *River of Dissolution* will be documented by page numbers in parentheses in my text.
2. D. H. Lawrence, *Lady Chatterley's Lover* (New York: Bantam Books, 1968), p. 301.
3. Frank Kermode, *D. H. Lawrence* (New York: Viking Press, 1973), p. 1.
4. Norman O. Brown, *Love's Body* (New York: Random House, 1966), pp. 221-22.
5. D. H. Lawrence, *Women in Love* (New York: Viking Press, 1960), p. 37. Subsequent quotations from *Women in Love* will be from this edition and will be documented by page numbers in parentheses in my text.
6. D. H. Lawrence, *Selected Essays*, "The Spinners and the Monks" (Harmondsworth, England: Penguin Books, 1950), p. 138.
7. D. H. Lawrence, *Sons and Lovers* (New York: Viking Press, 1968), pp. 353-54.
8. D. H. Lawrence, *The Rainbow* (New York: Viking Press, 1961), pp. 243-44.
9. D. H. Lawrence, *The Man Who Died* (New York: Random House, 1953), pp. 177-78.
10. Norman O. Brown, *Life Against Death: A Psychoanalytic Interpretation of History* (New York: Random house, 1959), p. 308.
11. D. H. Lawrence, *Phoenix II*, ed. by Warren Roberts and Harry T. Moore (New York: Viking Press, 1970), p. 574.
12. D. H. Lawrence, *Phoenix: The Posthumous Papers* (New York: Viking Press, 1972), p. 534.
13. *The Man Who Died*, p. 194.
14. See "Insouciance" (pp. 103-6) and "Sex versus Loneliness" (p. 15) in D. H. Lawrence, *Selected Essays*. See also Keith Sagar, *The Art of D. H. Lawrence* (London: Cambridge University Press 1966), pp. 225-26.
15. D. H. Lawrence, *Lady Chatterley's Lover*, p. 326.
16. D. H. Lawrence, *Selected Essays*, p. 213.
17. D. H. Lawrence, *Sex, Literature, and Censorship* (New York: Viking Press, 1959), p. 79.

18. D. H. Lawrence, *Lady Chatterley's Lover*, p. 351.
19. W.H. Davies, "Leisure," in *English Poetry in Transition: 1880-1920*, ed. John M. Munro (New York: Pegasus, 1968), p. 107.
20. *The Complete Poems of D. H. Lawrence*, edited by Sola Pinto and Warren Roberts (New York: Viking Press, 1971), p. 43.
21. Ibid., p. 716.
22. Ibid., p. 726.
23. Ibid., p. 720.
24. *Ibid., p. 727, 11.6-7.*

3
The Virgin and the Gipsy as Ironic Comedy

D. H. Lawrence's *The Virgin and the Gipsy* has received little critical attention partly because it is generally regarded as merely a dry run for *Lady Chatterley's Lover*. John B. Vickery has written discerningly but too briefly about myth and ritual in the story, F. R. Leavis has brought to bear his formidable arsenal of superlatives (" . . . it is one of Lawrence's finest things and is itself enough to establish the author's genius as major . . ."), and Julian Moynahan discusses it in the context of virgin heroines in the English novel tradition.[1] No one seems to have noticed however that *The Virgin and the Gipsy* possesses integrity as literature largely because of its comic character.[2]

One encounters comic features everywhere in the work. The principal figure, the virgin Yvette Saywell, is sympathetically teased throughout the story. This could be a dangerous enterprise, especially for an author supposedly incapable of the light touch. Yet in the following dialogue between our heroine and her sister Lucille, an exquisite comedy of virginal doubts, revulsions, and misgivings is enacted:

" 'What is it, Lucille,' she asked, 'that brings people together?. . . .' 'I suppose it's sex, whatever that is,' said Lucille. 'Yes, what is it? It's not really anything *common*, like common sensuality, you know, Lucille. It really isn't!' 'No, I suppose not,' said Lucille. 'Anyhow, I suppose it need not be.'. . . .'I *loathe* common fellows. And I never feel anything—*sexual*,' she laid a rather disgusted stress on the word, 'for fellows who aren't common. Perhaps I haven't got any sex.'

'That's just it!' said Yvette. 'Perhaps neither of us has. Perhaps we really haven't *got* any sex, to connect us with men!' 'How horrible it sounds: *Connect us with men*!' cried Lucille, with revulsion. 'Wouldn't you hate to be connected with men that way? O, I think it's an awful pity there had to *be* sex! It would be so much better if we could still be men and women, without that sort of thing.'

Yvette pondered . . . " [P. 81].[3]

"Perhaps I haven't got any sex, says Lucille, to which Yvette's "Perhaps neither of us has" indicates a comic range greater than, and dissimilar to, that generally found in Lawrence's treatment of female characters.

I wish, however, to consider *The Virgin* in the context of a theory of comedy formulated by Northrop Frye, because it supports my claim that this short novel is primarily comic by virtue of the ironic contrasts established within it by romance elements and literary analogues. According to Frye, "One pole of ironic comedy is the recognition of the absurdity of naive melodrama, or, at least, of the absurdity of its attempt to define the enemy of society as a person outside that society. From there it develops toward the opposite pole, which is the true comic irony or satire, and which defines the enemy of society as a spirit within that society."[4] It is thus a token of the sophistication of *The Virgin* that the enemy is located within. Indeed, the enemy occupies the seat of power, a fact again in accordance with Frye's specifications for comedy ("At the beginning of the play the obstructing characters are in charge of the play's society, and the audience recognizes that they are usurpers. At the end of the play the device in the plot that brings hero and heroine together causes a new society to crystallize around the hero . . . "—p. 163). That this crystallization does not occur in *The Virgin* accentuates its character as ironic comedy, and connotes in addition Lawrence's customary and significant open-ended resolution.

The Virgin and the Gipsy as Ironic Comedy

A glance at major relationships in the story will help to test the proposition that *The Virgin* is ironic comedy. The story presents four units in significant relation: (1) the older Saywells (the rector, Granny his mother, Aunt Cissie, and Uncle Fred; (2) the rector's two virgin daughters Yvette and Lucille; (3) Mrs. Fawcett and Major Eastwood (a recent divorcée and her lover); and (4) the gipsy. Fawcett-Eastwood and the gipsy could be placed in one category as they represent different aspects of the free, expressive life, and serve to increase the alternatives to conventional values concerning love and marriage. The rectory, citadel of the reigning power in *The Virgin*, represents the repressiveness and hypocrisy of conventional morality in familial form. The two girls are the prize they contest. Yet the comic-ironic dimension reinforces realism in avoiding the potential sensationalism of this situation. Instead of the gipsy confronting the rector in a battle of wills, the two men do not even meet. Instead of a set-to between the virgin protagonist, Yvette, and her antagonist father, in which the girl passionately announces her love for an outcast gipsy, their battle is caused by Yvette's misappropriation of money from a fund for the parish war dead initiated by the elder soured virgin Aunt Cissie. Yvette takes the money from the dead and gives it to the gipsy fortune-teller wife, money superstitiously cast to the forces of regeneration and vitality. But she lies about what she did with the money, and though her dishonesty does not imply a serious lapse of character, her father, always fearing the emergence of his passionate, deserting wife in his daughters, reacts as if she had had sexual intercourse with the gipsy rather than merely taken three pounds and thirteen shillings. The first "sexual gesture" toward the virgin arises in this scene, when, in reaction to her father's cold anger, Yvette feels "deflowered."

Irony appears again when the forces of liberation undermine one another. Yvette has met the gipsy in his camp while on an outing with some of her young friends. She comes under his "spell" and he becomes a part of her inner life, a new force to be engaged and assimilated. She returns to the gipsy camp (located, with appropriate primitiveness, in a quarry), where the following archetypal situation occurs: "At length his voice said, without breaking his spell: 'You want to go in my caravan, now, and wash your hands?'" Assenting to that old male gambit, Yvette "followed simply, followed the silent, secret, overpowering motion of his body in front of her. It cost her nothing. She was gone in his will." Things look very dark or very bright for our heroine (it could be either, so ostensibly neutral is Lawrence towards sexual initiaion in this story) when the whole plan is suddenly ruined by the chance approach of the other camp of rebels, the Fawcett-Eastwoods, who happen to be driving by and stop to warm themselves at the gipsies' fire. Moreover, some of the romantic mystery surrounding the Lawrentian dark god is dispelled (and thus the comic boundaries extended) when it turns out that the gipsy had served in Major Eastwood's own regiment.

Yet this Mellorsian gipsy (who, like the gamekeeper, is good with horses) is his own man, as character and as characterization. He disappears during the night after rescuing Yvette, and he speaks and writes a semiliterate English ("I come that day to say goodbye! and I never said it, well, the water give no time . . .") quite different from the cultured talk available to Lady Chatterley's lover. To cap the ironic treatment of his genuinely mysterious gipsy, Lawrence gives him the last name of a man given to pursuing professional nonvirgins and famous for possessing one of the classic "social" prose styles in English letters: Boswell.

But the supreme irony, which involves three central characters, Granny, Yvette, and the gipsy, and culminates in a profoundly unromantic embrace, occurs near the end of the story. The descriptions of Granny, the target of Lawrence's attack on English maternal domination, are comparable in revulsive power to Swift's Brobdingnagian gigantism:

> She sat there bulging backwards in her chair, impassive, her reddish, pendulous old face rather mottled, almost un-

The Virgin and the Gipsy as Ironic Comedy

> conscious, but implacable, her face like a mask that hid something stony, relentless. It was the static inertia of her unsavory power. . . . she was hibernating in her oldness, her agedness. But in a minute her mouth would open, her mind would flicker awake, and with her insatiable greed for life, other people's life. . . . [P. 19]
>
> That obese old woman, sitting there in her blindness like some great red-blotched fungus, her neck swallowed between her heaped-up shoulders and her rolling, ancient chins, so that she was neckless as a double potato, her Yvette really hated. . . . [P.96]

Granny further is compared to an old toad that swallows bees issuing from the rectory garden beehive. Such animalization of villainess and heroine provides another comic-satiric instance, and prefigures the gipsy and his successor, Lady Chatterley's gamekeeper, in a gardener who kills the toad for eating the bees.

If this treatment of Granny seems like excessive authorial hostility, Lawrence forcefuly describes her perniciousness:

> It was not as if the Mater were a warm, kindly soul. She wasn't. She only seemed it, cunningly. . . . Under her old-fashioned lace cap, under her silver hair, under the black silk of her stout, forward-bulging body, this old woman had a cunning heart, seeking forever her own female power. . . . The family was her own extended ego. Naturally she covered it with her power. And her sons and daughters, being weak and disintegrated, naturally were loyal. Outside the family, what was there for them but danger and insult and ignominy? [P.7]

Thus, Granny's presence at the climax of the relationship between the virgin and the gypsy structurally accords with the prototypic rules of Menandrine New Comedy by which the "senex," the obstructive elder, is finally removed. What brings hero, girl, and senex together in this story and removes the "senex" and "law" is a flood in the adjoining Papple river caused by the collapse of an ancient underground mine tunnel beneath the reservoir dam. The water assaults the rectory, drowning Granny before the eyes of Yvette and the gipsy and threatening to drown them as well. Driven by the swirling and mounting water to Yvette's bedroom (ironically the one safe place in this pious house), their first and last embrace keeps them from freezing to death. Indeed the final description in the flood episode is a grim travesty of orgasm:

> The vice-like grip of his arms around her seemed to her the only stable point in her consciousness. It was a fearful relief to her heart, which was strained to bursting. And though his body, wrapped round her strange and lithe and powerful, like tentacles, rippled with shuddering as an electric current, still the rigid tension of the muscles that held her clenched steadied them both, and gradually the sickening violence of the shuddering, caused by shock, abated, in his body first, then in hers, and the warmth revived between them. [P. 114]

Neither the gipsy's dark glamour, the force of the virgin's quest, nor the provocative presence of the rectory, can drive this hero and heroine into each other's arms; nothing but an "Act of God" can do it, and then not to consummate any grand passion, but to keep alive.

No less important than all the preceding ironic material in sustaining *The Virgin* as ironic comedy is the literary analogue. The first analogue is none other than "Mother Goose." Yvette has been invited out by her young, conventionally rebellious friends, but, typically errant, she turns them down. "She rather enjoyed being Mary-Mary-quite-contrary." Just as erratically she decides to go for a walk on a cold February day. The next day she goes cycling and ends up at the gipsy's camp where her sexual initiation is prevented only by the arrival of the Eastwoods. From the rector's standpoint, something "contrary" emerges in her gravitation toward both the gipsy and the Eastwoods, but we are also kept from taking Yvette too seriously by her extension into the submythic realm of Mother Goose land.

The Virgin and the Gipsy as Ironic Comedy

A more sinister analogue can be located in de Maupassant's little-known short novel *Yvette*. Here is a description of the home of this Yvette: "la maison de la mére est une maison publique dont la fille [Yvette] attire la clientèle."⁵ It is hard to be certain whether Lawrence read de Maupassant's *Yvette*, although we know from Rose Marie Burrell's *A Catalog of D. H. Lawrence's Reading from Early Childhood* that Lawrence read some of de Maupassant's "tales" in 1905.⁶ One is hesitant to regard the earlier story as an analogue if proof of Lawrence's acquaintance with the French *Yvette* is necessary (although Lawrence's choice of the same name for his heroine suggests that he might have known de Maupassant's *Yvette*.) But literary influence is of course often a subtle matter; Lawrence need have only heard about the other work. At any rate, a story about a French virgin named Yvette whose passage to maturity takes the form of realizing that her mother both runs a "high class" brothel and continues herself to take "lovers" offers a sharply contrasting background to Lawrence's virgin and the Saywell rectory.

The use of *Yvette* as an ironic foil to *The Virgin* takes on added value if we bear in mind Moynahan's arresting observation on the virgin in English literature: "The English virgin is an archetype through which that country's writers have expressed and reexpressed a communal ideal of the freshness and fullness of unimpeded life. Furthermore, the vicissitudes of the virgin in her successful avatars is always a revelation of the capacity of the society, at particular stages of development, to accommodate and embody this ideal" (p. 211). Comparing the two Yvettes in the light of these conceptions elaborates the nature of Lawrence's virgin. For if de Maupassant, after his virgin attempts suicide, has her cynically accept the world as a brothel, and life as a glittering cage (the famous "floating café" in *Yvette*, La Grenouillère, is an appropriate metaphor here) in which humans are trapped by their sexual drives, the resolution in Lawrence's story is something quite different. The French virgin submits to the viciousness of her society, reflecting de Maupassant's unpleasantly facile cynicism. Lawrence, however, with his Protestant transvaluative resistance to any social force threatening to corrupt the individual, rejects conventional society through as expressive a manifestation of the instinctual as one could encounter. A ferocious flood of life-redeeming water destroys the evil queen Granny (royal motifs pervade the story) and the rectory itself. Not only is the "senex" swept away, but the institutional image of the "law" that she embodies is demolished—a forceful indication that the enemy of society in this work is centrally internal and must be destroyed. It is a long way from the sensuous, amoral La Grenouillère to the dirty, cold, flooding Papple in Northern England—the distance between two visions of virginity, freedom, and captivity.

The last analogue, Tennyson's early "The Lady of Shalott," figures more complexly in *The Virgin* than the preceding two. Lawrence's Yvette is not merely a victim of Saywell tyranny and societal sanctions when compared to Tennyson's fated maiden. Indeed she has considerable freedom, as Lawrence openly states: "They were left so very free in their movements. Their parents let them do almost entirely as they liked. There wasn't really a fetter to break, nor a prison bar to file through, nor a bolt to shatter. The keys of their lives were in their own hands. And there they dangled inert" (p. 21). If Tennyson's virgin is a victim of mirrors and of mysterious magic malice ("A curse is on her if she stay/ To look down to Camelot/ She knows not what the curse may be"), Lawrence's Yvette is a victim of herself, experiencing a phase of a woman's growth (ll. 40-42). *The Virgin* then not only presents a comedy of antithetical moralities progressing toward a resolution, but the quirky, butterfly-like movement of humanity through the maze of virginity as well. To discern more clearly how the analogous qualities of the two works lend ironic and mythic stature to *The Virgin*, we will first consider the motifs of enchantment and mirrors in both.

A "magic" mirror is a pivotal image in "Shalott." By reflec-

The Virgin and the Gipsy as Ironic Comedy

ting what passes her on the road, the mirror reflects life. But reflection here means that the mirror creates illusion. Reality itself is a threat to Tennyson's virgin. The illusory reality of an enchanted condition marks her incarcerated range of experience. The virgin can survive only by remaining within her "spell"; the village churls and market girls and knights that pass by the enisled castle belong to a world denied her. If she looks at life directly (". . . look down to Camelot"), she will be destroyed. Because it is "bold Sir Lancelot" who finally compels the virgin to take the fatal glance at reality, dealings with the opposite sex are clearly taboo. In Tennyson's sentimental Arthurian pseudomythic world, virginity is a form of unavoidable sterility, but the alternative, the attempt to experience (let alone grow by) sexual relating, is forbidden. There's a curse against it, which can be interpreted to mean that society is emotionally attached to virginity as a permanent ideal, and that when a woman tries to leave it behind, she is anathematized by society.

The mirror in *The Virgin* does not crack from side to side when Lawrence's Lady of Shalott peers at her Lancelot. But she's a gazer too, and, like Tennyson's maid, dwells in a stone house isolated from reality by a river and stifled by a woman. (There is no evidence in the main analogue to Tennyson's poem, "The Fair Maid of Astolate," in Malory's *LeMorte D'Arthur*, that Elaine, the Maid, is under a curse by another woman, but Queen Gwynevere is jealous of her, thereby making this queen a comic double to the "queen" of the Saywell rectory, Granny.)

> At the first landing, she stood as she nearly always did, to gaze through the window that looked to the road and the bridge. Like the Lady of Shalott, she seemed always to imagine that someone would come along singing Tirralirra! or something equally intelligent, by the river. [P. 51]

But when the gipsy comes along by the river, he is screaming "run for your life!"

A mirror in *The Virgin* does bring latent antagonisms between the two sisters and the older Saywell woman to a head. A permanent rift has been made in the rectory by the rector's wife's leaving him for a more passionate man. The rector, attempting to recover from this shock, divides his wife into two people: "She-who-was-Cynthia," the "pure-white snowflower of his young bride," and the depraved creature who abandoned him. That a woman can be both "pure" and sexual provokes, of course, a familiar bewilderment in certain kinds of Christian mentality; embodied in the rector, this mentality results in one form of imprisonment from which the two sisters will suffer. Indeed, anything that smacks of "loose living" horrifies the rector, threatening his skin-deep liberalism and reminding him of his wife in her evil incarnation. This explains the fury he vents on Yvette when he discovers that his child has been mildly socializing with Eastwood and Mrs. Fawcett without his knowledge. Although the imprisonment of the virgin is partly internal, parental repression should not be underestimated as a force in the story. All the maniacal irritability that Aunt Cissie exhibits as a compensation for sacrificing her deeper self culminates in the rector's threatening to kill his daughter before allowing her to go the way of her mother.

The tension between the two sides of the family emerges then over a mirror that Yvette, in her typical state of virginal dazed carelessness, has perched on a piano and knocked off, almost breaking it. Ironically, it turns out to be Granny who is superstitious about cracked mirrors; in the Saywell house, a cracked mirror is not a sign of a doomed maid; a dropped mirror instead leads to a farcically unbecoming family squabble. Rather than either virgin being the victim of a spell or a prisoner in a magic castle, one of them is sent to her room for talking naughtily to Granny.

The parallels and the ironic contrasts continue. The "river's dim expanse" down which the body of the maid floats "deadpale between the houses high,/ Silent into Camelot" (11.157-158) becomes in *The Virgin* a "shaggy-tawny wave front of water advancing like a wall of lions" (P. 107). The class contrast between Malory-Tennyson's Lancelot and Lawrence's ironically pairs an aristocrat with a classless outsider. Whereas Elaine is the "outsider" in Tennyson's work, and Lancelot is on the inside and at the top of his society, Lawrence's gipsy is a pariah (except for his lower-class status as a horse groomer in the Army). Conversely, Yvette is an "insider," as a middle-class daughter of a clergyman ("There were plenty of young men to make love to her: even devotedly. But with impatience she had to shake them off. 'Why were they so unimportant?—so irritating!' " (p. 59)). If the Lady of Shalott is in a spell, "spell" operates as a key verbal motif to describe the semischizoid absentmindedness of Lawrence's virgin. She has, we are told early in the story, the "vague careless blitheness of She-who-was-Cynthia" (p. 5).

. . . she always seemed like a creature mesmerized. [P. 12]

Yvette absently grabbed another cake. [P. 18]

. . . Yvette was abstracted, agitated, hardly heeding: in one of her mesmerized states. [P. 31]

The gipsy may in some respects anticipate Mellors, but in this story he is literally and symbolically a forerunner of the flood. He is the spiralling force from the depths, which, like the flood, will jar her out of her spell and prepare her for mature relations. And to the degree that he is a symbolic extension of the libidinal energy represented by the flood, he can be said to destroy Granny (he doesn't, at any rate, attempt to save her as she is drowning), thus clearing away the largest obstacle to Yvette's emancipation.

If comedy, as Frye holds, embodies a progression toward reality, and a restoration of community, *The Virgin* partly qualifies as comedy while retaining Lawrence's regenerative inconoclasm. The Saywells have learned that the gipsy saved Yvette. A friend of the family wants the gipsy to be given a medal, and everyone thinks he should be thanked. But when they drive out to the quarry, the gipsy camp is no longer there. The Saywell family wants to render the communal inclusion of the "outsider," but he is not one to be included or even medalled. Society will have to restore itself without him. This possibility is embodied in the awakened girl, who, unlike the lady of Shalott, will not be "singing her last song."[7] The classical circle of comedy is completed in this story by an "existential" rather than a communal embrace. Tennyson's water moves a dead maiden towards reality; but Lawrence's water and dark lover destroy a part of society and shock the maiden into realization and maturation.

We will now turn to Lawrence at work resuscitating the "darkly lost" Etruscans in one of the last efforts of his career to merge personal life and death with society, and, in so doing, attempting to transcend the limits of the human condition.

Notes

1. John B. Vickery, "Myth and Ritual in the Shorter Fiction of D. H. Lawrence," *Modern Fiction Studies* 5 (1959-60): 77-78; F. R. Leavis, *D. H. Lawrence: Novelist* (New York: Simon & Schuster, 1969) p. 288; Julian Moynahan, *The Deed of Life: The Novels and Tales of D. H. Lawrence* (Princeton: N.J.: University of Princeton Press, 1963). R. E. Pritchard, on the other hand, regards parts of *The Virgin* as "squalid comedy" (*Body of Darkness*, p. 185). See also Mary Doyle Springer *Forms of the Modern Novella* (Chicago: University of Chicago Press, 1975) pp. 142-48) who describes *The Virgin* as having a "plot of learning" (p. 147).

2. M. G. Krishnamurti (in *D. H. Lawrence: Tale as a Medium* (Mysore: Rao and Raghaven, 1970)), detects a shade of comedy in Lawrence's novella ("The neutrality of tone which has an undercurrent of humour . . ." (p. 94).

3. All further references to *The Virgin and the Gipsy* are from the Bantam Books paperback edition (New York, 1968).

4. Northrop Frye, *An Anatomy of Criticism* (New York: Atheneum, 1957) p. 47.

5. Guy de Maupassant, *Contes Choisis* (Garden City, N.Y.: Doubleday, 1961) p. 252

6. Rose Marie Burrell, "A Catalog of D. H. Lawrence's Reading from Early Childhood," *The D. H. Lawrence Review* (Fall, 1970): 193-324.

7. Pritchard also discerns an apocalyptic, death-and-rebirth dimension in the story: "The inhuman flood is also death, occasioning rebirth. . . . The flood and the night together are apocalyptic, remembered by Yvette as 'the world's-end night.' She is reborn, in the words of the gypsy, 'braver in the body . . .' D. H. Lawrence: (*Body of Darkness*, p. 186).

4

D. H. Lawrence's Golden Age

They say the fit survive,
But I invoke the spirits of the lost.
Those that have not survived, the darkly lost,
To bring their meaning back into life again,
Which they have taken away
And wrapt inviolable in soft cypress-trees,
Etruscan cypresses.

Evil, what is evil?
There is only one evil, to deny life
As Rome denied Etruria
and mechanical America Montezuma still.
—from D. H. Lawrence's "Cypresses"

I

Although such students of D. H. Lawrence as Richard Aldington, Mark Schorer, Harry T. Moore, and Keith Sagar have attested to the high worth of Lawrence's last travel book, *Etruscan Places*, few have scrutinized the work closely or at length.[1] One of the exceptions is the English author Christopher Hassall who, in an essay read before the Royal

D. H. Lawrence's Golden Age

Society of Literature in 1959, discovers in *Etruscan Places* an esthetic for Lawrence's *Last Poems*: "The Etruscans provided him [Lawrence] with a group of symbols. Read in this light . . . his last travel book becomes his most revealing statement on the name and nature of poetry. . . . "[2] Hassall goes on: "Without first accepting him as a guide among the tombs of the dead we cannot properly experience the life in his last poems . . ."[3] Besides a poetic, Hassall excavates from *Etruscan Places* a source for Lawrence's acceptance of death. The word "excavates" is not chosen at random. For *Etruscan Places* in itself, like the sites and dead societies it describes, is a "site" to be excavated; much lies buried in it which should be dug up. Yet *Etruscan Places* is involved with life as well as death and paradoxically so. The book, written by a dying yet vividly alive man, celebrates a dead culture for its liveliness. R. E. Pritchard regards this paradox as "the transvaluation of life and death—upon which he had been engaged, from almost the beginning of his career—so that tomb and womb fuse together."[4]

Etruscan Places represents one of several of Lawrence's last works that ponder death and rebirth, Holy Dying and Holy Living. If in *The Man Who Died* the reader beholds an immortality for "the Man" (Lawrence's persona for himself and for our best selves) as a phallic Christ, or, in "The Ship of Death" a metaphor of life after death through an acceptance of self-oblivion, in *Etruscan Places* one witnesses literally the resurrection of an entire society from the tombs. The design of this chapter is to silhouette *Etruscan Places* against a background of Etruscological scholarship. This endeavor will reveal Lawrence's counterpoising two basic modes of personal and societal sensibility: a mechanical, power-oriented civilization (the Roman, and, by figurative extension, the "Roman"), and its antithesis, the organic, being-centered civilization (the Etruscan, or the "Etruscan"). I will also deal with Lawrence's travel book as the "tomb-womb" of an impressively humanistic esthetic, and as a kind of subjectivist or mythic thinking that Lawrence brilliantly expounds and identifies with the psyche of pre-Greco-Roman peoples.

Lawrence's interest in Etruria, as his interest in any place, was of course hardly that of a Baedeker. His description of place was always a definition of humanity: modern or ancient, rural or urban, Northern or Southern, cerebral or intuitive—the categories roll on, indicating the range of his preoccupations. Mark Schorer memorably expresses Lawrence's genius for place:

> . . . there is probably no other writer in literary history whose works responded so immediately to his geographical environment as Lawrence, and certainly there is no other modern writer to whose imagination 'place' made such a direct and intense appeal, and in whose works, as a consequence, place usurps such a central role. . . . Lawrence's people discover their identities through their response to place, and that, having thus come upon their true selves, they mark out their fate and are able to pursue it to another place—factory or farm, city or country, north or south, England or Italy, Europe or America, death or life.[5]

Lawrence certainly appears to have discovered an important part of his identity in Etruria, and even to have celebrated it. In the early summer of 1927, according to his wife Frieda, Lawrence had a lung hemorrhage.[6] Hans Carossa, an Austrian doctor and poet, examined Lawrence that fall, and declared that the average man in Lawrence's condition would have died years earlier.[7] Thus it is very possible that Lawrence, during the time of his visits to the Etruscan sites (April 6-10, 1927), knew that his own death was not far off. The Etruscan tombs, then, must have opened for him in more ways than one; what emerges is one of the ecstatic paradoxes of his life: a culture of gay movement, enlightened hedonism, and mysterious happiness conveyed through a sarcophagal context.

Much of Lawrence's significant work had been permeated by a concern with the second life: Paul Morel experiences through sex a new awareness of human unity with the natural

D. H. Lawrence's Golden Age

cosmos in the "peewits" scene with Clara in *Sons and Lovers*; Ursula Brangwen, after the "death" of the self that had loved the fragmented Skrebensky, is regenerated to a capacity to relate to men by the wild stallions near the end of *The Rainbow*; and central characters in *Women In Love* like Birkin and Ursula grope toward a new life of self-realization amid a disintegrating modern world. These deaths are obviously figurative, yet literally real enough too. But as Lawrence moves into the twenties, the specter of his own physical death looms up. And his search then no longer leads toward a "revolution in sensibility" by which to induce the death of the ego and the resurrection of a fulfilled self. Rather it becomes a quest for a more mystical experience of the descent into death and of survival, either through nature (as in the important late poem "Shadows"), through physical survival itself (which could be one facet of the lovely "dawn" passage in "The Ship of Death"), or, as in *Etruscan Places*, in a culture, which, confirming his own beliefs or hopes, envisaged death as a continuation of life. Thus this Etruscan conception held great excitement and authority for Lawrence; there it was, on the walls of the Tarquinia site, and elsewhere, not spelled but painted out, or molded in stonework: life after death, the life-in-death, was beautiful, ritualistic yet relaxed, gracious as a waterfall.

Lawrence knew what he was undertaking in entering his first Etruscan city, Caere (the modern Cerveteri), and in undertaking the ever-growing disciplined study of Etruscology. Archaeologists and scholars were already constructing and reconstructing conceptions of Etruscan civilization, working systematically with tomb artifacts to devise a scientifically accurate presentation of the Etruscans. But the room for doubt was large, and, although to a lesser extent, remains so. No one understood (nor understands today) the nature and structure of the Etruscan language. Therefore, the problem of origins made (and still makes) Etruscan identity a mystery: " . . .the great aim of contemporary Etruscan archaeology," says Raymond Bloch, a leading Etruscologist with field experience in Southern Etruria, "is to solve the enigma of Etruscan origins and the mystery of the language . . . and to establish the historical facts about the relations between the Etruscans and the Latins."[8] But the mystery of an attractive and obliterated people was meat for Lawrence's extraordinary imagination. His keenest interpretive energies went to work, deciphering images of animals into a symbolic bestial pageantry, manipulating recurring artifacts such as *cippi* (phallic posts or pillars), small stone ships, offering-dishes, mortuary sculpture and wall art into a formulation of a society, even of a lost cosmic sense. In one of the great imaginative projections in *Etruscan Places*, Lawrence envisages a society and mind impregnated with a religious vivacity:

> The natural flowering of life! It is not so easy for human beings as it sounds. Behind all the Etruscan liveliness was a religion of life, which the chief men were seriously responsible for. Behind all the dancing was a vision, and even a science of life, a conception of the universe . . . which made men live to the depth of their capacity.
> To the Etruscan all was alive; the whole universe lived; and the business of man was himself to live amid it all. He had to draw life into himself, out of the wandering huge vitalities of the world. The cosmos was alive, like a vast creature. The whole thing breathed and stirred. Evaporation went up like breath from the nostrils of a whale, steaming up. The sky received it in its blue bosom, breathed it in and pondered on it and transmuted it, before breathing it out again. Inside the earth were fires like the heat in the hot red liver of a beast. Out of the fissures of the earth came breaths of other breathing, vapours direct from the living physical under-earth, exhalations carrying inspiration. The whole thing was alive, and had a great soul, or anima: and in spite of one great soul, there were myriad roving, lesser souls; every man, every creature and tree and lake and mountain and stream, was animate, had its own peculiar consciousness. And has it today.
> The cosmos was one, and its *anima* was one; but it was made up of creatures. And the greatest creature was earth, with its soul of inner fire. [P. 49]

"To the Etruscan all was alive.... The cosmos was alive, like a vast creature .... every man, every creature and tree and lake and mountain and stream, was animate, had its own peculiar consciousness." All these animistic ideas climax in Lawrence's assertion that the Etruscans held "a conception of the universe ... which made men live to the depth of their capacity." Thus these ancient people figuratively embody Lawrence's abiding concern that men live religiously. "... Damn your happiness," says Paul Morel in *Sons and Lovers* during a crucial exchange with his mother about what is important in life, "So long as life's full, it doesn't matter whether it's happy or not" (p. 257, Viking Compass ed.). This is not only the young Morel-Lawrence speaking; it voices an older Lawrence. Intensity, vitalization, hylozoism (the ancient theory that all matter has life), the sundering of the wall between object and subject, human and other organisms: these gifts and others Lawrence would bring to Etruscology.

The hylozoistic idea of the earth itself as a deific being (to which Lawrence returns in *Apocalypse*) occupies a significant area of Old World sensibility that Lawrence would respond to and sensitively delineate. And not surprisingly, for both chthonic deities and animization of the earth incorporate appropriate concerns in a writer obsessed with recesses of impulse, instinct, and emotion. Lawrence asserts that "With the Egyptians and Babylonians and Etruscans, strictly there were no personal gods. There were only idols or symbols. It was the living cosmos itself, dazzlingly and gaspingly complex, which was divine ..." (p. 50). Although this animistic construction derives from John Burnet's *Early Greek Philosophy*, Lawrence creatively transmutes his borrowing. Lawrence will, for example, take the hylozoistic idea from the Milesian philosopher Anaximenes that "Just as our soul, being air, holds us together, so do breath and air encompass the whole world," (p. 75), or borrow the notion from Heraclitus that fire is the primary element of the universe (p. 146), then fire these antique conceptions into an exalting synthesis that renders the earth divine. In *Apocalypse* he admits that "Today, it is almost impossible for us to realise what the old Greeks meant by god or *theos*," (p. 84), a point corroborated by W. K. C. Guthrie's assertion that "We may never know exactly what was in Thales' mind when he said that all things were full of gods."[9] Even Bertrand Russell, not usually regarded as a religious enthusiast or fanatic, makes a point supportive of Lawrence's rapt hylozosim: "The metaphysics of Heraclitus, like that of Anaximander, is dominated by a conception of cosmic justice, which prevents the strife of opposites from ever issuing in the complete victory of either."[10]

Lawrence's thinking throughout *Etruscan Places* takes a spark from the "movement" and polarity philosophies of the pre-Socratic Greeks. Not only the concept of the prolific and the devourer found in *Last Poems*, but his animization of the universe in his last Italian travel book formulates in climactic mythic terms primitivist and "precognitive" elements found throughout his writings. Quoting Russell accentuates a point essential to supporting part of the virtue of *Etruscan Places*: that at least some of the conceptualization in that work is not simply fantasy or personal projection. Lawrence generally launches his hypotheses with those made by professional scholars in mind: " . . . it is not for me to make assertions. Only, that which half emerges from the dim background of time is strangely stirring; and after having read all the learned suggestions, most of them contradicting one another; and then having looked sensitively at the tombs and the Etruscan things that are left, one must accept one's own resultant feeling" (p. 20).

Prepared for objectivist strictures, Lawrence wages an attack throughout *Etruscan Places* against scientific standards of interpretation and evaluation. On the first page of the book, the great nineteenth-century German Classical historian, Theodor Mommsen, is chided for giving the impression that the Etruscans "hardly existed at all." "The Prussian in him," charges Lawrence, "was enthralled by the Prussian in the all-conquering Romans." Mommsen, in the five-volume *History*

D. H. Lawrence's Golden Age 75

of Rome, his greatest work, devotes twelve pages (and several scattered references) in an approximately 2500-page history to a people generally credited with supplying the Romans with many of the rudiments of their civilization: irrigation, architecture, social, political, and military organization, bronze-casting, and other arts, sports, and so on. Lawrence's charge is flat enough; Mommsen "didn't like the idea of them." Mommsen, unlike Lawrence, was definitely not attracted to the Etruscan religion: "The religion of the Tuscans in particular, presenting a gloomy fantastic character and delighting in the mystical handling of numbers and in wild and horrible speculations and practises, is equally remote from the clear rationalism of the Romans and the genial image-worship of the Greeks."[11] Despite these winning Classical allusions, the climax of Mommsen's highly scholarly and vivid history occurs in a powerful yet subtly disturbing idolization of Julius Caesar (a portrait with such striking similarities to George Bernard Shaw's Caesar as to indicate a sinister linkage between Mommsen's "complete and perfect man," the urbane Roman of *Caesar and Cleopatra*, and Shaw's later fondness for Mussolini and Stalin).

Lawrence is conversant with the literature abusing the Etruscans. Indeed part of the Etruscan "problem" is that the only contemporary records we have of this people come from the Greeks and Romans, who were as reliable about the "Tyrrhenians" as Russia or the United States would be about each other during the twentieth century to a historian in the year 4000 with only the literature of one country available. The Etruscans had a bad press from both contemporary and later commentators. The second-century (A.D.) Greek writer, Athenaeus, offers this lurid account of Etruscan viciousness from the two fourth century (B.C.) Greek historians:

> Among the Etruscans, who had become extravagantly luxurious, Timaeus in his first book relates that naked slave-girls wait on the men. And Theopompus in the forty-third

book of his *Histories* says that it is a custom among Etruscans to share their women in common; the women take very great care of their bodies and often exercise naked even with men, sometimes also with one another. . . . They are also terribly bibulous, and are remarkably beautiful. The Etruscans rear all the children that are born, not knowing who is the father in any single case. . . . It is no disgrace for Etruscans to be seen doing anything in the open, or even having anything done to them; for this, too, is a custom of the country.[12]

This description, which sounds like a Fellini filmscript fantasy, bears little resemblance to a society that endured for some six centuries. Where, one wonders, would these depraved voluptuaries have found the energy to build their hill-based walled cities, their handsome aqueducts, their metalwork? On the contrary, rather than frittering away their time and energy in extravagant license like the *Roman* set at Trimalchio's Banquet, they developed a dignified domestic culture. According to the Etruscologist Sibylle von Cles-Reden, the Etruscan woman was permitted "not only to attend festivals with her husband, but also to share responsibility for the management of the household, business, and landed property."[13] Alain Hus, another European Etruscologist, amplifies these points:

> The Tuscan family, as well as we are able to ascertain, constituted a living entity, based not only on religious and juridical foundations, but also on a real affection between the married couple, on one hand, and between parents and children on the other. In sum, the exact opposite of the picture drawn by Theopompus—much more modern and more warm-hearted than the Greek or Roman family. The woman, as wife and mother, played an important role. Without being a matriarchy, for the father remained head and guide, the Etruscan family was really centered around the woman. She enjoyed much freedom, appearing at banquets, and in public; husband and children accorded her great respect; she had a certain influence in business. . . . Very often the name of the woman figures in the ancestry of the dead, a practice unknown in Greece and Rome.[14]

According to the distinguished Italian Etruscologist and Italic archaeologist Massimo Pallotino, "the woman's place in Etruscan society was particularly high," an indication of social equality between the sexes.[15]

One source of stern condemnation of Etruscan political institutions can be traced to a man who seems nonetheless to have thought well enough of the Etruscans to write a twelve-hundred page book about them. This is the pioneer Etruscologist George Dennis, whose *The Cities and Cemeteries of Etruria*, published in 1883, Lawrence had read. Dennis, also an Englishman, had made a detailed and lively study of over fifty sites; Lawrence, knowing he was in no physical condition to compete with his fellow countryman, visited only four cities (although he said in a June 1927 letter to Earl Brewster that perhaps he and Frieda could soon do five more Etruscan cities, enough, as he put it, "for a book"). Perhaps the small number of sites covered also impelled Lawrence to be "subjective," to wield his material freely. Fortunately, Lawrence did visit one of the chief sites of Etruria, Tarquinia, an area regarded by a contemporary Etruscologist, Hugh Hencken, former Chairman of the American School of Prehistoric Research at Harvard, as a central location of and key to Etruscan civilization: ". . . such," says Professor Hencken, "was the importance of this city in Ancient Etruria that whatever was true of it might well have a wider application."[16] Another remark by Hencken bears on the fragmentary nature of Lawrence's Etruscan book: ". . . its [Etruria's] oldest and greatest cities in the heyday of Etruscan civilization were those along the coast, among them Caere, Tarquinia, Vuloi, Vetulonia, and Populonia."[17] The fact that Lawrence took in three of these five cities bolsters the representativeness of his visit. He would offer quality for Dennis's quantity.[18]

But Dennis's large and engaging work makes points about the political nature of Etruscan society worth mentioning in detail, because they constellate criticisms of the Etruscan polity at odds with Lawrence's interpretation and evaluation. According to the libertarian Dennis, "Political freedom was a plant which flourished not in Etruria. The power was wholly in the hands of priestly nobles; the people had no voice in the government. . . . The mass of the community was enthralled. . . . It is difficult to conceive a system of government more calculated to enslave both mind and body than that of the aristocratical augurs and aruspices of Etruria."[19] Yet shortly afterward Dennis asserts that "Etruria had a level of civilization second only to Greece. . . . [But] it could never have produced a Plato, a Demosthenes, a Thucydides, or a Pericles."[20] The response to that indictment of course is that not many other societies at any time have produced such a quartet (not to mention Homer, Aeschylus, Sophocles, Aristophanes, Aristotle, and some others). "The intellect of Etruria," concludes Dennis, in the brief anti-Etruscan section of his book, "was too much absorbed in the mysteries of divination and the juggleries of priestcraft."[21]

These constitute strong criticisms of Etruscan society, and, to a lesser degree, of Lawrence's evaluation of it and, as such, will in substance be used later to test Lawrence's testimony. However, I am not mainly concerned with proving something about the Etruscans; rather I wish to exhibit, analyze, and evaluate qualities of mind and imagination in *Etruscan Places* itself. But, as Lawrence says, "to the tombs, to the tombs!" It was not so easy to get to the tombs. The difficulties Lawrence encountered in transportation and accommodations may be judged by the following typical situation:

> We arrive at Palo, a station in nowhere, and ask if there is a bus to Cerveteri. No! An ancient sort of wagon with an ancient white horse stands outside. Where does that go? To Ladispoli. We know we don't want to go to Ladispoli, so we stare at the landscape. Could we get a carriage of any sort? It would be difficult!. . . . Meaning impossible. At least they won't lift a finger to help. Is there an hotel at Cerveteri? They don't know. . . . Well, we will leave our two bags at the station. But they cannot accept them. Because they are not locked. But when did a hold-all ever

lock? Difficult! Well then, let us leave them, and steal if you want to. Impossible! Such a moral responsibility! [Pp. 2-3]

Lawrence was also shadowed in Cerveteri by what might have been one of Mussolini's spies, who skulkily demanded identification. Recalling that Lawrence had coughed up blood shortly after his Etruscan jaunt, and that he had nearly died only two years before, one is all the more impressed by his rigorous style of travel. This is especially true on finding out that a multimillionaire named Lord Berners had offered to take him around the Etruscan cities in a Rolls Royce. But Lawrence was having none of that. In a February letter to his tomb-traveling companion, Earl Brewster, a New Englander and a student of Oriental philosophy, he rejects this luxury with misanthropic contempt: " . . . he's so rich. . . . It goes dead against my stomach. I simply *can't* stand people at close quarters. Better tramp it our two selves."[22]

Led by shy or ignorant guides—"I asked the boys what they called it [a wild mignonette]. They gave the usual dumbbell answer; 'it is a flower,' " and by his own sharp instincts and empathetic intelligence, Lawrence is charmed by the Cerveteri vaults: "They are surprisingly big and handsome, these homes of the dead. Cut out of the living rock, they are just like homes" (p. 9). And, a few pages later, "The tombs seem so easy and friendly. . . . One does not feel oppressed, descending into them. It must be partly owing to the peculiar charm of natural proportion which is in all Etruscan things of the unspoilt, un-Romanized centuries" (p. 12). After a little more description, Lawrence moves into a typical generalization:

> The things they did, in their easy centuries, are as natural and easy as breathing. They leave the breast breathing freely and pleasantly, with a certain fullness of life. Even the tombs. And that is the true Etruscan quality: ease, naturalness, and an abundance of life, no need to force the mind or the soul in any direction.

And death, to the Etruscan, was a pleasant continuance of life, with jewels and wine and flutes playing for the dance. It was neither an ecstasy of bliss, a heaven, nor a purgatory of torment. It was just a natural continuance of the fullness of life. Everything was in terms of life, of living [P.12].

This progression from specific impression to evaluative generalization represents a pattern as integral to the shape of the book as its rhythm and polemic irony of contrasting the lively past with the moribund present.

It is in a Cerveteri site that Lawrence encounters the little bronze ship of death that is to lead to his greatest poem, "The Ship of Death," and, in other verse in his *Last Poems*, to an impressively serene attitude toward death. This ship of death passage culminates in another remarkable sequence in *Etruscan Places*, and intimates one of the central propositions underlying the entire book. First, Lawrence takes the ship to symbolize a Noah's Ark, which he then interprets as an " . . . Ark, the *arx*, the womb. The womb of all the world. . . . the ark of the covenant, in which lies the mystery of eternal life . . ." (p.14). The interpretation gathers momentum: "And perhaps in the insistence on these two symbols [the arx and the phallus, represented in the tombs as *cippi*], in the Etruscan world, we can see the reason for the utter destruction and annihilation of the Etruscan consciousness.

> The new world wanted to rid itself of these fatal, dominant symbols of the old world, the old physical world. The Etruscan consciousness was rooted quite blithely in these symbols, the phallus and the arx. So the whole consciousness, the whole Etruscan pulse and rhythm, must be wiped out.
> Now we see again, under the blue heavens where the larks are singing in the hot April sky, why the Romans called the Etruscans vicious. Even in their palmy days the Romans were not exactly saints. But they thought they ought to be. They hated the phallus and the ark, because

they wanted empire and dominion and, above all, riches: social gain. You cannot dance gaily to the double flute and at the same time conquer nations or rake in large sums of money. [P.14].

II

This passage introduces the two structural themes in *Etruscan Places* of the Old World and power. Lawrence's handling of both matters is overtly, even combatively, ideological; each ideological; each comprises part of what is great in this last "travel" book. Lawrence is conjecturing when he states that the Etruscans "were, we must feel, of an old, primitive Mediterranean and Asiatic or Aegean stock" (p. 19). In the continuing contemporary debate, uncertainty still exists whether the Etruscans were immigrants from Asia Minor or autochthons, so Lawrence's guess is not rash. Nor does the following seem outrageously "subjective": "The Etruscan civilisation seems a shoot, perhaps the last, from the prehistoric Mediterranean world, and the Etruscans, newcomers and aborigines alike, probably belonged to that ancient world" (p. 19). Dr. Cles-Reden, discussing Etruscan religious culture, partly corroborates Lawrence on this hunch, twenty-eight years later: " . . . the bright daylight of Olympus, resting on the presupposition of an abstract detachment from death, never dawned over this world, which remained rooted in the primitive, narrow earth-cult of the Mediterranean's pre-Indo-European period."[23]

Lawrence enlarges on this Old-World idea in another book, in his Foreward to *Fantasia of the Unconscious:*

> I honestly think that . . . the great pagan world which preceded our own era, once had a vast and perhaps perfect science of its own, a science in terms of life. . . .
> I believe that this great science previous to ours and quite different in constitution and nature from our science once

was universal, established all over the then existing globe. I believe it was esoteric, invested in a large priesthood.²⁴

Then, after the melting of the glaciers, the world flood, and the fleeing of refugees from the drowned continents to the high places, Lawrence continues, ". . . some, like Druids or Etruscans or Chaldeans or Ameridians or Chinese, refused to forget, but taught the old wisdom, only in its half-forgotten, symbolic forms."²⁵

After furnishing us with an Old World, factitious or otherwise, Lawrence in *Apocalypse* projects the sensibility of the ancient period:

> . . . we have not the faintest conception of the vast range that was covered by the ancient sense-consciousness. We have lost almost entirely the great and intricately developed sensual awareness, or sense-awareness, and sense-knowledge, of the ancients. It was a great depth of knowledge arrived at direct, by instinct and intuition, as we say, not by reason. It was a knowledge based not on words but on images. The abstraction was not into generalisations or into qualities, but into symbols. And the connection was not logical but emotional. The word 'therefore' did not exist. Images or symbols succeeded one another in a procession of instinctive and arbitrary physical connection—some of the Psalms give us examples—and they 'get nowhere' because there was nowhere to get to, the desire was to achieve a consummation of a certain state of consciousness, to fulfill a certain state of feeling-awareness.²⁶

Whether the Etruscans, Babylonians, Egyptians, Chaldeans and others thought like this or not, one can recognize in this passage a sensitive presentation of an order of cerebration, and, more specifically, a kind of thinking that one associates in modern literature with the Symbolists and Imagists. (It also resembles the esthetic of transcendent self-realization of the Japanese Noh or Dance drama so admired by William Butler Yeats.) This passage then dovetails into his idealization of the Etruscans for their naturalness and spontaneity. "The desire . . . to achieve a consummation of a certain state of consciousness" is however less Symbolist or Lawrentian doctrine than a "strange mode of being," and one of those striking perceptions of creative sensibility that Lawrence would hit upon throughout his career.

That the Etruscans may have thought in a mode different from and earlier than their Greek and Roman contemporaries is also suggested by Pallotino in a passage from Seneca: "The difference between us [i.e., the Graeco-Roman world] and the Etruscans . . . is the following: that whereas we believe lightning to be released as a result of the collision of clouds, they believe that clouds collide so as to release lightning (for as they attribute all to the deity, they are led to believe not that things have a meaning insofar as they occur, but that they occur because they must have a meaning) . . ."[27] The cause-and-effect form of Classical thinking is strikingly different in kind from the "magical" mode of thought of the Etruscans, who here resemble Ur-Symbolists. Assuming the form of effect-cause, Etruscan thinking would hardly lead to the great rationalist tradition of Western Civilization. Yet in establishing another realm of meaning and in putting lightning at the apex of their inquiry, Etruscan thought represents a vitalist, numinous mentality that Lawrence found preferable to the literalist reductionism inherent in the major tradition.

Lawrence locates the source of this pre-Hellenic sensibility in what he calls an old cosmic religion: "Myths, and personal gods, are only the decadence of a previous cosmic religion" (*Etruscan Places*, p. 109). He relates Etruscan artifacts to an interpretation of that religious culture so unappetizing to Dennis and Mommsen:

> The strange potency and beauty of these Etruscan things arise, it seems to me, from the profundity of the symbolic meaning the artist was more or less aware of. The Etruscan religion, surely, was never anthropomorphic: That is, whatever gods it contained were not *beings*, but symbols of elemental powers, just symbols: as was the case earlier in

Egypt. The undivided Godhead, if we can call it such, was symbolised by the *mundum*, the plasm-cell with its nucleus: That which is the very beginning; instead of, as with us, by a personal god. . . . (PP. 66)

Lawrence's formulation of an ancient-world psyche deserves attention for what light it may cast on both the Etruscans and the pre-Hellenic peoples generally. This psyche is very possibly relatable to a period that, ending at the point where Ionian philosophy is assimilated by the culture of Classical Greece, moves backwards into Cretan, Egyptian, Babylonian-Mesopotamian civilizations culminating in the early and imposing Sumerian society. A quotation from H. G. Wells' *The Outline of History* extends a period, which, Wells feels, has been misleadingly contracted:

> The time that elapsed between the empire of Sargon I and the conquest of Babylon by Alexander the Great was as long, . . . at the least estimate, as the time from Alexander the Great to the present day. And before the time of Sargon, men had been settled in the Sumerian land, living in towns, worshipping in temples, following an orderly Neolithic agricultural life in an organized community for at least as long again.
>
> One of the most difficult things for both the writer and student of history is to sustain the sense of these time-intervals and prevent these ages becoming shortened by perspective in his imagination. Half the duration of human civilization and the keys to all its chief institutions are to be found *before* Sargon I.[28]

If Lawrence is correct in his conjecture that the Etruscans *are* remnants of peoples living prior to the Graeco-Roman epoch, and very different from that epoch in sensibility, then we possibly behold in the Etruscans an anachronism of something like an Old-World mind stretching from early in the first millenium B.C. to the third millenium B.C. and perhaps further back. The issue of Etruscan origins is still sufficiently unresolved to permit the speculation that the Asiatic origin theory that places them on the island of Lemnos (near

Asia Minor) would also have brought the Etruscans into contact with other civilizations of the Near East, such as Mesopotamia and surrounding smaller coastal nations like Lydia and Phrygia, and even Egypt. The American Etruscologist Emeline Richardson provides support in regard to Etruscan linguistic origins: "Though it is still imperfectly deciphered, modern scholars have recognized that the Etruscan language is non-Indo-European and connected with other Eastern Mediterranean languages of a non-Indo-European, pre-Hellenic character."[29] And the Italian Etruscan scholar Luisa Barti holds that "Modern scholars have modified Herodotus's theory of a Lydian origin, for under the influence of possible relationships and comparisons, the Etruscans have been related to far distant zones of Asia Minor, Armenia and Mesopotamia."[30] Pallotino also sees indications of a remote background: "The monuments of ancient Etruria . . . are closer to this second class of archaeological remains . . . ," the "megalithic temples of prehistoric Malta."[31]

Lawrence's pronouncements about the Etruscan psyche become even more cogent from corroborative information offered by Henri Frankfurt:

> The ancients, like the modern savages, saw man always as part of society, and society as embedded in nature and dependent upon cosmic forces. For them nature and man did not stand in opposition and did not, therefore, have to be apprehended by different modes of cognition. . . . natural phenomena were regularly conceived in terms of human experience and . . . human experience was conceived in terms of cosmic events. . . .
> The fundamental difference between the attitudes of modern and ancient man as regards the surrounding world is this: for modern scientific man the phenomenal world is primarily an 'It'; for ancient--and also primitive--man it is a 'Thou'.[32]

Frankfurt's claim that ancient man had an "I-Thou" relationship with the external world is strikingly similar to the sense permeating some of the Lawrence's works of an integral relatedness between human beings and other entities, inorganic as well as organic. That this condition applied to more than Mesopotamian civilization is borne out by the American Egyptologist John Wilson: "The phenomenal world to him was not 'It' but 'Thou.' It was not necessary that the object become finally superhuman and be revered as a god before it might be conceived in terms of 'Thou'. . . . The Egyptian might—and did—personify almost anything: the head, the belly, the tongue, perception, taste, a tree, a mountain, the sea, a city, darkness, and death."[33] Although the Egyptian and Mesopotamian mind may not have constituted the whole ancient mind, it certainly comprised a large part of it, especially if we realize that Mesopotamia is often used as a very broad term to designate civilizations ranging from early Sumeria down to people like the Chaldeans and Persians who were coeval with the Graeco-Roman and Etruscan world.

Thus evidence indicates that this Old World sensibility was not just a figment of Lawrence's "imagnification." It was a form of speculation, and speculation, says Frankfurt, "is an intuitive, an almost visionary, mode of apprehension. This does not mean, of course, that it is a mere irresponsible meandering of the mind, which ignores reality . . ."[34]

Lawrence's vitalism again seems virtually duplicated in another description by Frankfurt of the mind of the "primitive" person: "Any phenomenon may at any time face him, not as 'It,' but as 'Thou.' In this confrontation, 'Thou' reveals its individuality, its qualities, its will. 'Thou' is not contemplated with intellectual detachment; it is experienced as life confronting life, involving every faculty of man in a reciprocal relationship. Thoughts, no less than acts and feelings, are subordinated to this experience."[35] Lawrence of course would have scorned the verdict that a human being is primitive because he discerns more life in his relations with the environment and the universe than Western thought would allow. One of the more startling insights in *Etruscan*

Places springs from Lawrence's notion that Western man has violated himself in trying to manipulate rather than relate to nature. The result of such a violation is a kind of compensatory punishment:

> The old religion of the profound attempt of man to harmonise himself with nature, and hold his own and come to flower in the great seething of life, changed with the Greeks and Romans into a desire to resist nature, to produce a mental cunning and a mechanical force that would outwit Nature and chain her down completely . . . till at last there should be nothing free in nature at all. . . . Curiously enough, with the idea of the triumph over nature arose the idea of a gloomy Hades, a hell and purgatory. To the peoples of the great natural religions the after-life was a continuing of the wonder-journey of life. To the peoples of the Idea the after-life is hell, or purgatory, or nothingness, and paradise is an inadequate fiction. [*Etruscan Places*, pp. 75-76]

This passage perhaps comes closer than any other in *Etruscan Places* to a concise summation of Lawrence's ideas about antithetical modes of the imagination and the fusion of literal and figurative ideas of death and rebirth in mythic terms. Even the abiding Lawrentian dedication to an ideal fulfillment is there, expressed in the pre-Classical language of flux ("great seething of life").

Some of the poems from *Last Poems* provide further material for contemplating Lawrence's evocation of the ancient mind. One might read "Mana from the Sea" for example as a "Lawrentian" exercise in sensibility ("Lawrence's acute sensitivity to watery nature"), but doing so obscures the poem's true cosmos. If, however, we put the poem in the context of the ancient faculties of imagination explored in this chapter, then what Lawrence articulates becomes something broader than a verse by an eccentric genius:

Do you see the sea, breaking itself to bits

against the islands
yet remaining unbroken, the level great sea?

Have I caught from it
the tide in my arms
that runs down to the shallows of my wrists,
 and breaks
abroad in my hands, like waves among the
 rocks of substance?

Do the rollers of the sea
roll down my thighs
and over the submerged islets of my knees
with power, sea-power
sea-power
to break against the ground
in the flat, recurrent breakers of my two
 feet?

And is my body ocean, ocean
whose power runs to the shores along my arms
and breaks in the foamy hands, whose power
 rolls out
to the white-treading waves of two salt feet?

I am the sea, I am the sea!

One notices in the second stanza the obliteration of the object-subject division basic to rationalist, causative thought. The great outer world and its force become, in the "experiencer" in the poem ("persona" being too passive a word for this occasion), one with the "sea" within him. Yet the poem goes beyond being simply a watery analogy between world and man, for both are seen as being water and land ("the sea, breaking itself to bits against the islands" and "the tide in my arms . . . that breaks abroad in my hands"), thus destroying the wall between objective and subjective modes of apprehension. As, further, "the tide in my arms" suggests the movement of blood through the body, Lawrence's commingling of modes takes on the authority of a physiological fact boldly translated into subjectivity.

But there is a larger purpose here that can be glimpsed synoptically by considering the first two lines of the poem and then its final line. The first two lines present a conventional objective description, a clear-cut separation between the speaker and the sea scene he is viewing with someone else. But by the final line of the poem, the poles of object and subject have coalesced, the world in the poem turned inside out. What was There is now Here, the speaker-experiencer has so deeply engaged the external world as to become one with it in a paean concretized in the details of mergence spread throughout the poem. Thus "I am the sea!" is not a Romanticist poet growing lyrical at getting his toes wet in the surf. Lawrence in this late poem has subtly performed a transformation of sensibility more fully appreciated if the poem is taken as approximating an Old World mentality. Although perhaps no one will ever prove that Lawrence's speculations about the ancient psyche are fully valid, the evidence suggests that his preternatural empathy might indeed have recrystallized an archaic form of thought.

III

Closely tied to Lawrence's theorizing about the Old World is the issue of power. In a recent study called *Lawrence's Bestiary*, Kenneth Inniss neatly poses a problem about power in *Etruscan Places* that deserves a hearing. According to Professor Inniss, " . . . Lawrence remained capable of falsifying his blood response, of ignoring his case against force, insisting that, in accordance with the mystical duality founded in nature and recognized in the animal motifs of the tombs, Roman 'wolves' were, in effect, divinely appointed to destroy Etruscan and other 'deer' so as to keep a metaphysical balance."[36]

Inniss's point is based on a conceptual passage in *Etruscan Places* in which Lawrence interprets some of the animals seen in the *Tomba delle Iscrizioni* (The Tomb of the Inscriptions) in the Tarquinia site. Lawrence, after describing the animals for several pages, pairs them off into symbolic dualities: "The leopard and the deer, the lion and the bull, the cat and the dove, or the partridge, these are part of the great duality, or polarity of the animal kingdom" (p. 56). Then he ventures an interpretation that is intriguing because one cannot be sure how much of it reflects Lawrence's own vitalism, and, with Burnet and Frankfurt in mind, how much accurately describes values from an Old World culture. "But they [the paired animals] do not represent good action and evil action. On the contrary, they represent the polarised activity of the divine cosmos, in its animal creation" (p. 56).

The consummation of this meditation occurs shortly after in another of those keen-imaged conceptual sequences that makes this little book based on mortuary artifacts so curiously exhilarating:

> The deer or lamb or goat or cow is the gentle creature with udder of overflowing milk and fertility; or it is the stag or ram or bull, the great father of the herd, with horns of power set obvious on the brow, and indicating the dangerous aspect of the beasts of fertility. These are the creatures of prolific, boundless procreation, the beasts of peace and increase. So even Jesus is the lamb. And the endless, endless gendering of these creatures will fill all the earth with cattle till herds rub flanks all over the world, and hardly a tree can rise between.
> But this must not be so, since they are only half, even of the animal creation. Balance must be kept. And this is the altar we are all sacrificed upon: it is even death; just as it is our soul and purest treasure.
> So, on the other hand from the deer, we have lionesses and leopards. These, too, are male and female. These, too, have udders of milk and nourish young; as the wolf nourished the first Romans: prophetically, as the destroyers of many deer, including the Etruscans. So these fierce ones guard the treasure and the gateway, which the prolific ones would squander or close up with too much gendering. They

D. H. Lawrence's Golden Age

bite the deer in neck and haunch, where the great bloodstreams run.

So the symbolism goes all through the Etruscan tombs. It is very much the symbolism of all the ancient world. [P.57]

Thus, if the devouring beasts occupy a necessary role in the cosmic drama of man and nature, why should the Roman "wolves" be censured in *Etruscan Places* (as they are continuously)? This contradiction would appear to be intensified by Lawrence's own linking of the wolves and the Romans in the above quotation. Nevertheless, Lawrence's point that the Etruscans would be "devoured" sooner or later reinforces the esthetic and metaphysic underlying the entire book. His strident (and libertarian) dislike for the Roman wolves is a prejudice that amounts to a conflict between a portion of his metaphysics and his political passions. But what Lawrence has to say about Roman power and Etruscan liveliness is far more basic to *Etruscan Places* than his prolific-devourer (or deer-wolf) metaphysic, which serves a relatively minor function in the book. This consideration can be illuminated from another perspective by discussing the two antithetical forms of power dramatized in the work.

These can simply be called the Roman and the Etruscan modes of power. From the first to the last pages of *Etruscan Places*, Lawrence inveighs against the Roman mode. Indeed, in the very first sentence of the book, he describes the Romans as the annihilators of the Etruscans, "the inevitable result of expansion with a big E, which is the sole *raison d'être* of people like the Romans" (p. 1). Shortly after, Lawrence, in a sharply libertarian indictment, insists that the Romans "smashed nation after nation and crushed the free soul in people after people . . ." (p. 2). And near the end of *Etruscan Places*, the influence of "Romanism" is visible in signs of Fascism and Mussolini in Volterra, one of the chief towns in northern Etruria. Brewster and Lawrence are given the Fascist salute by some impudent Volterran girls (they do not return it). Lawrence spots a message painted on a town wall:

"Mussolini ha sempre ragion!" Says a Lawrence strikingly different from the creator of Ramon and Cipriano, in *The Plumed Serpent*, completed only two years before: "Some are born infallible, some achieve infallibility, and some have it thrust upon them" (p. 100).

Between the beginning and the end of *Etruscan Places*, and comprising some of its major passages, emerges the theme of Roman power time after time, rendered all the more terrible by contrastive juxtaposition with the Etruscan mode. Besides being imperialist, the Roman mode is brutal and insensitive. In a 1920s speech, Mussolini expresses this mode unencumbered by "parliamentary" obliqueness: "Our programme is quite simple; we wish to rule over Italy. People are always asking us about our programme. There are too many already. Italy's salvation does not depend on programmes but on men and strong wills."[37] The Etruscan mode is the opposite:

> It is all a question of sensitiveness. Brute force and overbearing may make a terrific impact. But in the end, that which lives lives by delicate sensitiveness. If it were a question of brute force, not a single human baby would survive for a fortnight. It is the grass of the field, most frail of all things, that supports all life all the time. But for the green grass, no empire would rise, no man would eat bread: for grain is grass; and Hercules or Napoleon or Henry Ford would alike be denied existence.
> Brute force crushes many plants. Yet the plants rise again. The Pyramids will not last a moment compared with the daisy. And before Buddha or Jesus spoke the nightingale sang, and long after the words of Jesus and Buddha are gone into oblivion the nightingale still will sing. Because it is neither preaching nor teaching nor commanding nor urging. It is just singing. And in the beginning was not a Word, but a chirrup.
> Because a fool kills a nightingale with a stone, is he therefore greater than the nightingale? Because the Roman took the life out of the Etruscan, was he therefore greater than the Etruscan? Not he! Rome fell, and the Roman phenomenon with it. Italy today is far more Etruscan in its pulse than Roman: and will always be so. [P.29]

This is the sort of unfettered generalizing that makes some Etruscologists (and experts in general) grumble about the wild flights of amateurs. But it is an inspiring passage of ethical and esthetic transvaluation, stunning in its tenderness, and relevant to all ages and places. To be sure, one might be under duress if compelled to prove that these two antithetical power modes describe with complete accuracy the history of political and military relations between the Romans and the Etruscans. For one thing, the Etruscans were themselves a potent military force. They ruled Rome during most of the sixth century. They were regarded as the chief naval force in the western Mediterranean during Rome's early days, and, as already indicated, effectively blocked Greek expansion in Italy. "It was Etruria," says Pallotino, "that first gave the Italic peoples the urge to conquer and dominate the sea."[38] The sea west of Italy was named after them (the Tyrrhenian, *Tyrrhene* being Greek for Etruscan; the Etruscans referred to themselves as the *Rasna* or *Rasena*, while "Etruscan" comes from the latin *Etruscus*), a sign of their maritime supremacy. Furthermore, the Etruscans themselves were quite willing to do a little colonizing up and down the Western central reaches of Italy.

Yet when one thinks of the concentration of political, military, and economic energy that goes into establishing and perpetuating an imperium, the Romans certainly outweigh the Etruscans in the power scales. Lawrence was justified in setting up the Romans as the more power-willed of the two societies, even if we might feel that Roman civilization exemplified considerably more for posterity than oppression, domination, and belligerence.

In the "sensitiveness" passage, and in other power passages, Lawrence develops a Roman power-image rich in associations. Lawrence in the Roman mode of power symbolizes the mechanization of private and social experience and the brutalization of other peoples easily associable with certain modern states. "War is the health of the State," Randolph Bourne used to say, and, we add today, one of the illnesses and still the possible death of the world body. Lawrence's "Roman" power stands for an impulse the institutionalization of which, as H-bombs, concentration and slave-labor camps, and profit-or-victory-at-all-costs standards attest, threatens the foundations of civilization and of human perpetuity itself.

But what about the Etruscan power mode, which Lawrence associates with vitality, with life? Mystical, religious, it was saliently a vertical power structure in which priest-kings (*Lucumones* or *Lucumos*) rule over society:

> The people are not initiated into the cosmic ideas, nor into the awakened throb of more vivid consciousness. Try as you may, you can never make the mass of men throb with full awakenedness. They *cannot* be more than a little aware. So you must give them symbols, ritual, and gesture, which will fill their bodies with life up to their own full measure. Any more is fatal. And so the actual knowledge must be guarded from them, lest knowing the formulae, without undergoing at all the experience that corresponds, they may become insolent and impious, thinking they have the all, when they have only an empty monkey-chatter. The esoteric knowledge will always be esoteric, since knowledge is an experience, not a formula. But it is foolish to hand out the formulae. A little knowledge is indeed a dangerous thing. No age proves it more than ours. . . .
> The clue to the Etruscan life was the Lucumo, the religious prince. Beyond him were the priests and warriors. Then came the people and the slaves. People and warriors and slaves did not think about religion. There would soon have been no religion left. They felt the symbols and danced the sacred dances. For they were always kept *in touch*, physically, with the mysteries. The 'touch' went from the Lucumo down to the merest slave. The bloodstream was unbroken. But 'knowing' belonged to the high-born, the pure-bred. [Pp. 51-52]

This important passage, which develops from the vitality-of-the-cosmos quotation, is essential in evaluating the justification of power and the Etruscan social structure displayed in *Etruscan Places*. The entire power passage (including the "natural flowering of life" section) is difficult to evaluate because it intertwines imaginative speculation about a "primitive" religious mind and idea of community and the universe, with a patronizing and elitist polity.[39] "A little knowledge is a dangerous thing." So two alternatives are implied: to give the "masses" no knowledge at all, or to give them more than a little. Lawrence selects the first. Give them "symbols, ritual and gesture," he says; the esoteric knowledge, the knowledge behind the veil of "mystery, miracle, and authority" will repose in the benevolent, wise, but firm grasp of the *Lucumones*, Etruscan-Lawrencean-Dostoevskian Grand Inquisitors. In his preface to "The Grand Inquisitor" Lawrence scolds Dostoevsky for making the Inquisitor appear to be such a villain for extolling these three qualities: ". . . let the specially gifted few make the decision between good and evil, and establish the life-values against the money-values. And let the many accept the decision, with gratitude, and bow down to the few, in the hierarchy. What is there diabolic or satanic in that?"[40] Lawrence's *Apocalypse* also contains elitist strains, reminding us that his tenderness literature of the late 1920s did not really end his attachment to concepts of leadership. His theory of an Elect shows a brazen perspicacity. Perhaps many people in most societies have been incapable of absorbing sophisticated or complex knowledge; as Lawrence puts it (and he means more than cognition), few men can attain to "full awakenedness" and "more vivid consciousness."

The deep dissatisfaction one feels toward this aspect of Lawrence centers upon the ideal of becoming, one of the cardinal values of both the Western revolutionary democratic ethos of the last two centuries and the Judeo-Christian tradition of moral transformation. What so many documents and events surrounding this value—*The New Testament*, the French Revolution, the Declaration of Independence, the Spanish Civil War, the numerous Nationalist struggles for liberation and *self*-expression—shared was perhaps the only remaining popular religious belief of our epoch: that all human beings deserved the opportunity, economically, politically, socially, and educationally, to develop their potential selfhood and humanity. Perhaps not all, possibly even many, would fail to do so; they deserved the chance nevertheless. Kenneth Rexroth, beautifully expressing a communal sense of the self, in effect contravenes Lawrence's elitism:

> Each of us is a specific individual, that one and no other, out of billions. I think each of us knows his own mystery with a knowing that precedes the origins of all knowledge. None of us ever gives it way. No one can. We envelop it with talk and hide it with deeds.
> Yet we always hope that somehow the others will know it is there, that a mystery in the other we cannot know will respond to a mystery in the self we cannot understand. The only full satisfaction life offers us is this sense of communion.[41]

In all fairness, Lawrence has said more than once that he supports, or, more accurately, tolerates, political and economic democracy. In the essay "Democracy," he asserts that "Democracy and Socialism rest upon the Equality of Man, which is the Average. And this is sound enough, so long as the Average represents the real basic material needs of mankind."[42] And even *Women in Love's Lucumone*, Rupert Birkin, offers, if grudgingly, an individualistic democratic code of a bizarre sort:

> But I, myself, who am myself, what have I to do with equality with any other man or woman? In the spirit, I am as separate as one star is from another, as different in quality and quantity. Establish a state on *that*. One man isn't any better than another, not because they are equal, but because they are intrinsically *other*, that there is no term of comparison. The minute you begin to compare, one man is seen to be far better than another, all the inequality that you can imagine is there by nature. I want every man to have his share in the world's goods, so that I am rid of his importunity. . .[43]

Lawrence encompasses Birkin, but Lawrence too did compare, did accept and think in terms of hierarchies of superior and inferior people. Some of this constitutes the golden egg of his strange art, and can be praised. The character in a Lawrence fiction living (or not living) in a coagulated, one-track self is clearly "inferior" to the one whose behavior symbolizes an effort to merge consciousness and instinct (we overlook the point that Lawrence's unfortunate phrase, "blood-consciousness," accentuates *awareness* of one's deeper, darker self, not only, even not primarily an exaltation of the sensibility of the unconscious for itself; the term, after all, is not "blood-*un*consciousness"). One is troubled less by Lawrence's hierarchies than by his caste rigidity and absoluteness. Man in this frame remains the slave of his birth. This proclivity in Lawrence's thought becomes absurd when Lawrence describes a *Lucumone* visiting an Etruscan town and populace, utterly awing them ("the people derive strength even from looking at him"), then passing on in his regal robes, "divine," "seated silent within another world of power, disciplined to his own responsibility of knowledge for the people...." [P.59]

A miner's son, Lawrence himself is a living contradiction of his own social and class snobbery. Had it not been for a series of nineteenth-century educational reform acts, which, as Frank O'Connor has observed, opened the schools up to a larger number of traditionally underpriviledged and undereducated English youths, Lawrence would not have been exposed to the books and ideas and people that contributed to his self-realization as one of the great literary artists of the twentieth century.[44] Would *he* have been content with "symbols, rituals, and gesture?" As an Etruscan miner's son in a society guided by a Lawrentian polity, Lawrence would have danced and played the double flute on Sundays and dug and crouched in the mines of Populonia on the other six days.

Is there any merit in Lawrence's idealization of the

Etruscan caste polity, of the Etruscan power mode? A writer like Anthony Powell in his urbane and elegant *roman fleuve*, *A Dance to the Music of Time*, is repelled by the increasing immorality, dislocation, and vulgarization of the modern social order. Although it would be erroneous to identify Lawrence as a champion of the upper class in the manner of Powell or of a Yeats, one can easily trace in some works of Lawrence a rooted belief in the rule or authority of the superior. The criteria of this superiority are not always clear, but his "*Lucumones*" often resemble himself, whether as Birkin in *Women in Love*, Ramon in *The Plumed Serpent*, Lilly in *Aaron's Rod*, the Man in *The Man Who Died*, or Mellors in his prophetic moments in *Lady Chatterley's Lover*.

A frequently invoked criterion is vitality, a paramount value in Lawrence's work generally, and a term that flashes in and out of the tombs in *Etruscan Places*. The problem with vitalism understood in the broader, nonphilosophical sense is less its subjectivity than its relativity. Is the poet, or the muscular prizefighter, the more vital person? Is the "*Lucumone*" a person with sensitivity or with great physical strength? The prizefighter, demolishing the poet by his own standards of superiority and achievement, would declare himself the more vital of the two. And only poems would survive to contradict him. Lawrence gets around this problem partly in the fool-killing-a-nightingale passage already quoted, but the problem remains. A vitalist ethic can always be brutalized into an ethic or a regime of force and oppression, the Antonines succeeded by a Mussolini (or worse).[45] And an elitist dynasty can degenerate in a very short time, so that within decades an ignorant, mass population is saddled with the enlightened rule of a Nero or a Commodus (the son of Marcus Aurelius). The Etruscan and the "Roman" modes of power, instead of necessarily forming a polarity, can become identical.

Lawrence's account of the Etruscan polity does, however, acquire strength and cogency from embodying not only his

D. H. Lawrence's Golden Age

own (partly contestable) values, but from being an inspired guess about the real nature of the Etruscan social structure. All Etruscologists agree that it was an intensely religious society, but not exactly Judeo-Christian. Alain Hus delineates the Etruscan religious characater vividly:

> The idea of sin had no place among them, the only sanction of an act was its success or its failure, both determined by Fate and justified by the accomplishment or non-fulfillment of certain rites. Deprived thus of freedom, the Etruscan passionately followed his fundamental instinct in which he recognized a superior principle. This is the root of his predilection for the most exuberant forms, baroque, sensual, or affective music, frenzied dances, indeed, even the cruelty revealed in his nature. From this stems too his taste for the ephemeral, the instantaneous, for realism. . . . From this also comes his attitude towards sexual questions, at the basis of which must be seen, not vice or license, but the exaltation of natural pleasure and the life-principle itself . . .[46]

IV

A key term in testing further the moral and ethical quality of the Lawrentian-Etruscan polity is a famous word in Lawrence's last writings: touch. Lawrence, defending the Etruscan social order, states that the leaders always kept the people "in touch" physically with the sacred mysteries, through dance, ritual, and symbolic object. This touch, Lawrence continues, "went from the Lucumo down to the merest slave. The blood-stream was unbroken" (p. 52).

Lawrence is really describing two matters in this passage: his representation of a communal (or close-knit, cooperative) society, and his theory of "blood-consciousness," the phallicism he was to dramatize and celebrate in his work of the late twenties. I will take up the motif of phallicness first, for it too is central to *Etruscan Places*.

One does not have to read far into this book to realize that these Etruscans embody one of Lawrence's most elaborate attempts to project an image of the "dark-gods," his chthonic agents of an ideal intuitive, sensitive life. He had dramatized these gods in English Midlands miners, dark-skinned peoples of Southern Europe and American, and animals like snakes and horses and whales. But, before *Etruscan Places*, he had not seized upon an entire nation to incarnate the "passional" full life. Even better, Etruria was a past society with so little left by and about it by which to reconstruct an authoritative history, that the imagination could move freely over the material. Lawrence looked closely (so many people, he used to say, look but never see) at the Tarquinian wall paintings, terra-cotta and stone sculpture at Caere and Vulci, at Volterran ash-chests, and envisaged a phallic people. Indeed, the men were even painted a "dark" color, vermillion ("Vermilion is the colour of his sacred or potent or god body," Lawrence suggests, bringing together associations from the American Indian, ancient Roman (possibly Etruscan) kings, and "Ezekiel" on the princes of Chaldea) (p.42). But the phallicism ascribed by Lawrence to the Etruscans is chiefly important because of an esthetic that he derives from it.

First a word about the *cippi* is in order. The *cippi* were not sexual hallucinations by the author of *Lady Chatterley's Lover*. The mild and rather ascetic Brewster confirms Lawrence's response by likening the *cippi* to the *lingam* he had recently observed at Hindu temples in India. To verify further the sexual, phallic nature of the *cippi*, one notices that they are invariably decorated with such masculine symbols as warriors, lions, and other combative power-beasts. The presence of symbolic penises at Etruscan sites should not be surprising, in view of our knowledge of the general recurrence of sexual symbols in ancient Mediterranean cultures. What does catch the eye is the dramatic, bold example of the "womb-tomb" feature of Etruscan culture: artwork of a flam-

D. H. Lawrence's Golden Age 101

boyant penis undismayed by death and its trappings, and of the womb-*arx*, sexual sources of the living universe.

Describing a burial vault at Cerveteri (Caere), Lawrence says: "It is the natural beauty of proportion of the phallic consciousness, contrasted with the more studied or ecstatic proportion of the mental and spiritual Consciousness we are accustomed to" (p. 10). An antithetic doubling of esthetics comprises one facet of this esthetic: pyramid vs. nightingale, empire versus grass, Word versus chirrup, stone versus painted wood. And, in regard to the institutionalization of art, the opposites are Etruscan places and museums. According to a respected British Etruscologist, David Randall-MacIver, who published one of his books on the Etruscans the same year Lawrence published his, "Many a long day might be spent on wandering and dreaming about the site of Veii [an Etruscan town near Rome], but apart from the romance of the spot and its historic interest the student will learn more from the contents of the excavations shown in the Museo di Villa Guilia [in Florence]."[47] But for Lawrence, who *had visited* Etruscan collections in museums in Florence, Rome, and other locations, the museum is the esthetic keystone of all the ponderous, dehumanizing monumentality in civilization that stifles, instinct, growth, chance, "impulse from a vernal wood." The "Roman" conception of life discloses a vision of dull perpetuity and mechanization, which in Lawrence's *Last Poems* figures as a recurring metaphor of circularity; concepts (and facts) such as empires, dynasties, and legions are false eternities in space (or place), time, and power. Museums, storehouses of past cultures and art (often "acquired" by victorious invaders), are the esthetic equivalent of the "Roman way." "Museums anyhow are wrong. But if one must have museums, let them be small, and, above all, let them be local . . . how much happier one is in the museum at Tarquinia, where all things are Tarquinian, and at least have some association with one another, and form some sort of *organic* whole" (p. 27). Lawrence here sounds much like Paul and Percival Goodman in their book *Communitas*; a certain respect for human scale and appropriateness of setting is, he feels, violated by the large, impersonal museum that symbolizes the repository for a ravishment of "place." A museum is deader than a tomb, at least, an Etruscan tomb.

Deader than any sort of tomb, Lawrence infers, are the scholars and scholarship incorporating the "book-museums" filled with erudition unenlivened by imagination. Lawrence develops this implication comically in his description of a young German scholar with whom he tours the Tarquinian tombs one day: "*Nicht viel wert* . . . doesn't amount to anything—seems to be his favorite phrase, as it is the favorite phrase of almost all young people today. Nothing amounts to anything, for the young" (p. 63). Lawrence essays an ambitious interpretation of the Tomb of the Bulls (the "mundum" passage), but, he says, " . . . the youth will have nothing of this. He is a modern, and the obvious alone has true existence for him" (p. 67). The German

> . . . has been in Sicily and Tunis, whence he has just returned; didn't think much of either place—*mehr Schrei wie Wert*, he jerks out, speaking as if he were throwing his words away like a cigarette-end he was sick of; doesn't think much of any place; doesn't think much of the Etruscans—*nicht viel wert*; doesn't, apparently, think much of me; knows a professor or two whom I have met; knows the tombs of Tarquinia very well, having been here, and stayed here, twice before; doesn't think much of them; he is going to Greece; doesn't expect to think much of it. [p. 63]

One cannot help being stirred by the complexity of the persona Lawrence projects in all four of the travel books, written as they were under a variety of circumstantial pressures and states of mind. This subject could form a lengthy essay in itself; it will suffice to say here that Lawrence's own passionate empathy towards exotic or ancient cultures did not in the least hamper his full responsiveness to his immediate social environment. Its potential humor, pathos, human or imaginative insufficiency he registered continually while retaining an identity as an author or an Englishman Abroad sharply different from the "Lawrence" of, for example, *Sons and Lovers* or *Look! We Have Come Through!* Lawrence treats the German youth humanely—"One can't blame the young. . . . The war cancelled most meanings for them" (p. 63)—but also as a representative of the scientific, rationalist mind, uprooted from the deeper being possible in a more coherent age. As such, he becomes, like the Lawrentian Maremma shepherd who appears earlier in *Etruscan Places*, a character in a drama of Past versus Present, and mythic versus cognitive mind.

The museum (or anti-museum) motif culminates late in the book in a highly implicative passage. Observing some sixty alabaster ash-chests in a famous Volterran tomb known as the Inghirami Tomb and "reconstructed" in a room of the archeological museum at Florence, Lawrence offers an insight which Etruscologists might ponder before using "amateur" and "subjectivist" too freely as terms of abuse:

. . . if this tomb is really arranged as it was originally, and the ash-chests progress from the oldest to the latest counterclockwise, as is said, one ought to be able to see certainly a century or two of development in the Volterran urns.
But one is filled with doubt and misgivings. Why, oh why, wasn't the tomb left intact as it was found, where it was found? The garden of the Florence museum is vastly instructive, if you want object-lessons about the Etruscans. But who wants object-lessons about vanished races? What one wants is a contact. The Etruscans are not a theory or a thesis. If they are anything, they are an *experience*.
And the experience is always spoiled. Museums, museums, museums, object-lessons rigged out to illustrate the unsound theories of archaeologists, crazy attempts to co-ordinate and get into a fixed order that which as no fixed order and will not be co-ordinated! It is sickening! Why

must all experience by systematized? Why must even the vanished Etruscans be reduced to a system? [P. 114]

This passage among other things indicates Lawrence's acute responsiveness to the plastic arts and to the integrity of place as archaeological setting. Nor is Lawrence being an antiintellectual dumbbell in opposing scholarly categorization of knowledge and experience. His negative attitude to scholarly systematization is significantly qualified: "Why must *all* experience by systematized?" Some, he implies, has to be, some best not be. One recalls the familiar but abiding unhappiness in academia that vitalness can evaporate in the classification of experience to which professional intellectual endeavor is committed.

Lawrence does make Etruscan society an experience, and anyone who like Bertrand Russell indicts him as a protoNazi worshipper of brutal instinctuality, must come to terms with this passage and others in *Etruscan Places* that celebrate quality over quantity, and sentience over classification. Lawrence is harsh with archaeologists, but that is tit for a future tat. A bigger issue obtained, and obtains: the "struggle between the endless patience of life and the endless triumph of force." A respect for integrity of place, (which ultimately means man's "place" in a place), becomes a complex cultural gesture; art and politics become one. Lawrence's esthetic now assumes larger proportions: "Give us things that are alive and flexible, which won't last too long and become an obstruction and a weariness" (p. 26). Art, creeds, social and political conception of order and governance, buildings, memorialized deeds, language—none of these matters should become media for or agents of the "Roman" power quest, of the drive to a spurious permanence. In accepting finiteness and transience, the brief beauty of the brightly painted, terra-cotta wood edifice or the supple fecundity of grass, one accepts both life *and* death, and is not, so Lawrence's argument would run, driven to eternalize himself in museum, church, or imperium out of a fearful rejection of death.

We are familiar with Lawrence's esthetic of transience in his poetry and fiction, but it is also formulated strikingly in his "Preface to the American Edition of New Poems," published in 1920. An exaltation of the *now* is contrasted with what Lawrence designates as the poetry of the past and of the future: "Life, the ever-present, knows no finality, no finished crystallization. The perfect rose is only a running flame, emerging and flowing off, and never in any sense at rest, static, finished."[48] The protototalitarian esthetic of Richard Wagner is pertinent here. To simulate a condition of absolute audience "captivity," Wagner wanted all the doors and exits of an opera house locked and bolted during a performance of his operas. A politics resides within both Lawrence's wood-and-grass esthetic and Wagner's of bolted opera doors. Without making too much of the authoritarian implications of Wagner's esthetic, one can take hold of Lawrence's as further evidence of that impetuous, freewheeling libertarianism so curiously interwoven into his elitist tendencies. A lyrical affirmation of authentic experience and of the necessity and beauty of finiteness should not easily lapse into a totalitarian vision of society. Lawrence's Etruscan polity might be hieratic in ways sharply distasteful to a democratic modern, but his sense of the *human* dimensions of art and social structure is too profoundly imbued with two favorite words of his last years, touch and tenderness, to categorize Lawrence rightly as a Fascist.

The subjects of touch and tenderness convey one to the most intimate regions of the polity and esthetic broached in *Etruscan Places*, and of Lawrence's other important writings of this period as well. "Tenderness," we recall, was one of the alternate titles for *Lady Chatterley's Lover*, and embodies a controlling motif and theme in that novel. Whether Mellors is convincing or not as an ideologue, tenderness is a tenet in his manifesto. Repeatedly connected with touch, tenderness is consummated in sexual intercourse: "Sex is really only touch, the closest of all touch. And it's touch we're afraid of. We're only half-conscious, and half-alive."[49] And, shortly after, in a passage which Lawrence might better have omitted but is at least useful ideologically, Mellors says (to himself):

> 'I stand for the touch of bodily awareness between human beings . . . and the touch of tenderness. And she is my mate. And it is a battle against the money, and the machine, and the insentient ideal monkeyishness of the world. And she will stand behind me there. Thank God I've got a woman. . . . ! And as his seed sprang in her, his soul sprang towards her too, in the creative act that is far more than procreative.[50]

In *Lady Chatterley's Lover*, the entire industrialized society is "Roman," and Connie and Mellors are possibly the last Etruscans. And in *Etruscan Places* itself, in a famous passage on Etruscan painting, Lawrence's perception about art can also be viewed as a definition of "Etruscan" sensual awareness: "The Etruscan artist seems to have seen living things surging from their own centre to their own surface" (p. 68). Affection, said Lawrence somewhere else, is a middle-class emotion; it is not from the "centre."

A very different kind of touch occurs in *Women in Love*. There the joining of touch to a perverse desire to know helps the willful Gudrun to reduce her "unutterable enemy" Gerald: "She wanted to touch him and touch him and touch him, till she had him all in her hands, till she had strained him into her knowledge" (p. 324). The "centripetal" direction of Gudrun's energy and intent contrasts completely with the center-derived tenderness of Lawrence's positive love scenes. Lawrence is not simplistically affirmative in writing about touch.

Touch-and-tenderness are entertained in another context in the late essay "Apropos of *Lady Chatterley's Lover*". Here Lawrence argues against domination of one human being by another, and establishes communion on a functional level seldom noticed in Lawrence's writings: "The great river of male blood touches to its depths the great river of female blood—yet neither breaks its bounds. It is the deepest of all

D. H. Lawrence's Golden Age

communions, as all the religions, in practice, know. And it is one of the greatest mysteries, in fact, the greatest, as almost every initiation shows, showing the supreme achievement of the mystic marriage."[51]

The conception in this quotation of a definition of community based on sensual and organic closeness is crucially important in an age accused, as ours is, of atomizing human relationships. The vision of a society that attempted to relate people to one another as an I-Thou establishes a conception of "Etruscan" community as reciprocal self realization. This fulfillment stands in total opposition to the "Romanization" of society and the world. In order to keep perspective, though, we must remind ourselves, as Lawrence fails to do, of the immersion in and abuse of power by the Etruscans themselves. The French Etruscologist Jacques Heurgon presents testimony that any just evaluation of the Etruscans would need to consider:

> . . .it is evident that the mining industry which, in Populonia and in the Campiliese, was the foundation of Etruscan power, had to fall back on a large amount of slave labor. . . . Juvenal describes the punishments meted out to those pampered and indolent city slaves when they misbehaved. They were sent into darkest Lucania to labor in the fields, or in *Tusca ergastula* (the Tuscan slave prisons). . . . there must have been in Populonia, at the mouth of the Po, and in the Etruscan campagna, *ergastula* of this nature—hutments or vaults in which miners were locked for the night, or labourers engaged in draining the marshes. But the life led in these places was so atrocious that 'ergastulum' became a synonymn for 'slave prison,' in which there were prisoners . . . whose manacles were never loosed.[52]

This evidence would seem to detract from Lawrence's picture of a happy society. The charge might be mitigated by considering that it comes from a Roman (though a great satirist), and that it might refer to the period of decline in Etruscan history that began late in the sixth century with certain important military defeats. We should also weigh Pallottino's remark that "Attempts at revolution on the part of the lower classes must have been rare, and so came to be remembered as particularly sensational events, as for example the revolution at Volsinii [a major Etruscan city]".[53]

Another aspect of the Etruscan esthetic is incorporated in their religious practise of divination. It harmonizes with the larger purpose of this essay that divination is secondarily defined in Webster as "unusual insight or intuitive perception." To give an idea of the special quality of Lawrence's descriptive-interpretive writing from another angle, I want to contrast his treatment of the ancient art of augury (or divination) practised by the Etruscans with an account by Raymond Bloch:

> The doctrine of orientation, which lies behind Etruscan interpretation of thunder and lightning, is fundamental to the art of the *haruspex*. For the Tuscans, the consecrated object is—as it were—an image of the universe. In the animal offered to the gods, the liver, the seat of life, reflects the state of the world at the moment of sacrifice. On its surface, the priest distinguishes the seat of the gods and, according to the configuration of the parts connected with each god, he can foretell the future. The bronze liver of Piacenza, which is divided into divine compartments in this way, is a microcosm. And the application of the principle of orientation creates a correspondence between the scrutiny of the sky, of the thunder and lightning and of the victim's liver.[54]

Now here is Lawrence, at the point of tranforming an impression of the "Tomb of the Inscriptions" at Tarquinia into one of his "metainterpretations":

> Birds fly portentously on the walls of the tombs. The artist must often have seen those priests, the augurs, with their crooked, bird-headed staffs in their hand, out on a high place watching the flight of larks or pigeons across the quarters of the sky. They were reading the signs and

portents, looking for an indication, how they should direct the course of some serious affair. To us it may seem foolish. To them, hot-blooded birds flew through the living universe as feelings and premonitions fly through the breast of a man, or as thoughts fly through the mind. In their flight the suddenly roused birds, or the steady, far-coming birds, moved wrapped in a deeper consciousness, in the complex destiny of all things. And since all things corresponded in the ancient world, and man's bosom mirrored itself in the bosom of the sky, or *vice versa*, the birds were flying to a portentous goal, in the man's breast who watched, as well as flying their own way in the bosom of the sky. If the augur could see the birds flying *in his heart*, then he would know which way destiny too was flying for him. . . .

. . .if you live by the cosmos, you look in the cosmos for your clue. If you live by a personal god, you pray to him. If you are rational, you think things over. But it all amounts to the same thing in the end. . . . All it depends on is the amount of *true*, sincere, religious concentration you can bring to bear on your object. An act of pure attention, if you are capable of it, will bring its own answer. And you choose that object to concentrate upon which will best focus your consciousness. [Pp. 54- 55]

"An act of pure attention": this of course is not only an Old World form of apprehension; it is a state of mind for writing a poem, for pondering the possibility of having another child or for taking a new job. "Divination," says Lawrence, helped Columbus discover America.

Lawrence expands on augury for almost two pages, evolving his thought in the sort of expansive generalization and applicability typical of these "nodal" passages. These comparisons are not meant to suggest the superiority of subjective to objective writing (or vice versa) on a lost culture. Rather they are intended to exemplify personal, subjective prose of a high order, as well as to show that room exists for both kinds of writing on complex and controversial subjects. Lawrence is more judgmental than Bloch (and all Etruscologists I have read) on the meaning of Etruscan artifacts, and his interpretation becomes evaluative in the process of humanizing augury.

He brings it home to us, whereas Bloch, through the demands of professional objectivity, keeps his subject at a distance—from subjectivity and from the reader. It was a distinguished student of ancient history and Etruscologist, H. H. Scullard, who stated that "Etruscology is not a topic which easily breeds unanimity of opinion."[55] Professor Scullard particularizes the controversial nature of Etruscan studies in respect to subjectivity: "In assessing such factors as the religious mentality or attitudes to life of a people whose literature does not survive to speak for them, judgment is likely to be subjective."[56] Such significant admissions did not prevent Scullard from entirely overlooking *Etruscan Places* (an omission more excusable in continental scholars like Heurgon and Cles-Reden who might not know English—although both Bloch and the ubiquitous Pallotino indicate appreciative awareness of Lawrence on the Etruscans).[57]

Lawrence's passage on divination also accentuates the "artistic" propensity of the Etruscans by underlining a doctrine of correspondences similar to the *Symboliste* one of modern literature. But unlike the modern Symbolist esthetic, divination, a central Etruscan religious practice and part of the code of rituals and observances known as the *Disciplina Etrusca*, evidences the intense, if "superstitious," immersion of the Etruscans in the natural environment.[58] Like Lawrence, they were keen observers of their surroundings; conversely, Lawrence is Etruscan in his vital perceptiveness of "birds, beasts, and flowers," earth and sky.

V

All the insights, brilliant guesses, and sympathetic interpretations in *Etruscan Places* constitute a form of wisdom writing concerning how to take life and death *in the present*. Lawrence exhibits both a mystical subtlety and a courageous practicality about the problem of death utterly foreign to what passes for practicality among modern people. How does one approach death? This absorbing theme and its profoundly human practicality as a subject in *Etruscan Places* compensate for another difficulty with the ideology in that piece. Lawrence's Etruscans were an intuitive, libidinal, pleasure-oriented people. By his (affirmative) standards, they were not very ego-oriented, not concerned with survival (although their obsession with prophecy makes one partly demur). If so, this would account for their failure to form an adequate confederation (Mommsen's "Prussian"-"Roman" indictment) against more collectivist, or confederative, aggressors like Rome, or formidable vandals like the Gauls. A social order based on pleasure (even if not on the level of Athenaeus's polymorphous perversity), on an ethic of vitality or even vitalism, on a wise "blood-consciousness," is not enough. It is a weakness that recurs in theoretical areas of Lawrence's work: an unsatisfactory treatment of the energies and restraints required for a stable political community in harmonious conjunction with a libertarian conception of the self and of the communal relationship. The problem is evaded rather than resolved by converging an integrity of self with a vitalist principle of societal leadership in the person of a Don Ramon, a Lilly, a Lawrence.

Lionel Trilling in *Sincerity and Authenticity* sets forth a powerful individualistic formulation of the relation of self and society:

> . . . there is one point of connection between the two men [Rousseau and Wordsworth] that requires to be kept in mind—the passionate emphasis each of them put upon the individual's experience of his existence. Rousseau calls this . . . the 'sentiment of being.' Wordsworth calls it by the same name. It figured in their minds, as it did in Walt Whitman's who said that it is 'the hardest basic fact and only entrance to all facts.' The facts to which this fact is entrance are those of the social and political life—it is through our conscious certitude of our persoonal selfhood that we reach our knowledge of others.[59]

Trilling here endorses some aspects of Lawrence's "culture"

of the self, by implying that the relation between self and society ("others") need not be only antagonistic. Lawrence, too, was if anything concerned with the "sentiment of being." The thrust of Trilling's book, as of Freud's *Civilization and its Discontents*, is toward elaborating an idea of the tragic, ineluctable disharmony of self and society. Lawrence addressed himself to this disharmony too, although his treatment at its worst seems either politically reactionary or too extreme in its individualism, or, as a recent student of Lawrence, Baruch Hochman, has it, too inconclusive:

> Like Jung, moreover, he [Lawrence] is unable to deal theoretically with the rackling tension of the human animal, who is perceived to be trapped between the claims of history, the urgencies of self and the urgencies of society, and who can maintain both integrity and understanding by acknowledging heroically the tragic dividedness of his own nature. As a consequence, like Jung but unlike Freud, he oscillates between an atomistic sense of the radical claims of the pre-conscious, pre-social self in its isolation, and a totalitarian sense of the validity of civilization.[60]

Worth citing against this indictment is an important point by Raymond Williams: "The living, organic, believing community will not be created by standing aside, although the effort towards it in consciousness is at least as important as the material effort."[61] The implication here that *any* valuable novelistic rendition of individual consciousness possesses positive social attributes needs to be remembered in social criticism of Lawrence. We have so accepted the Freudian definition of tragedy as to verge on being close-minded toward ideas at variance with it. Birkin, the Ursula of *The Rainbow*, Tom Brangwen, Connie Chatterley and Mellors may not represent typical human beings, but they are people whose experiences and responses to life in varying degrees inform us about new possibilities of personal sensibility *and* social culture. Lawrence's profound attempt to enrich consciousness

D. H. Lawrence's Golden Age

well outweighs solipsistic or totalitarian tendencies in his work.

To dismiss *Etruscan Places* as escapist is a serious error. The work is a Golden Age parable. It discloses Lawrence's dwelling happily in an Arcadia less rural and naive than, but as much a great dream as, that of another inspired sensibility:

> 'Happy times and fortunate ages were those that our ancestors called golden, not because gold (so prized in this our Iron Age) was gotten in that happy era without any labors, but because those who lived then knew not those two words *thine* and *mine*. In that holy age all things were in common, and to provide his daily sustenance all a man needed to do was to lift up his hand and pluck his food from the sturdy oaks that generously invited him to gather their sweet, ripe fruit. The clear fountains and running brooks offered him bountifully their refreshing waters. In the clefts of the rocks and in the hollow of trees the busy, provident bees fashioned their republic, offering without interest the fertile harvest of their fragrant toil to every hand. The robust cork trees, inspired by their own courtesy alone, divested themselves of their broad light barks, with which men began to cover their houses built on rough stakes, using them only as a defense against the inclemencies of heaven. All there was peace, all friendship, all concord. The heavy share of the curved plow had not dared to open and expose the compassionate bowels of our first mother, for she without compulsion offered through all the parts of her fertile and spacious bosom whatever could nourish, sustain, and delight the children who possessed her.[62]

Neither Don Quixote nor Lawrence is renowned for his acceptance of quotidian reality; both were out of place or alienated in their time; both are Utopists in the extreme pressure of their sense of what human life should be. Quixote presents an equalitarian, primitively communistic, blissful Paleolithic Arcadia, and Lawrence a delightfully poised hieratic society filled with people who seem as pre-Freudian as dolphins. *Both* men are demented?

Surely the half-crazed, convulsed character of much of contemporary society, of what Trilling would describe as our modern inauthenticity of being, is made bearable and, one hopes, transformable, by the incessant and unfathomable energies of the ideal. What is ideality, for all its possible interlinkage with narcissism or escape or even madness, but the faith that life has been and again will be beautiful and gracious and free-moving? And what more significantly practical than Lawrence's realization, the "tragic" lesson of Gibbon's *The Decline and Fall of the Roman Empire*, that nothing lasts, all things (good and bad) perish, and one finds images and symbols of a satisfying society where one can? The majestic authority of Lawrence and of the Cervantes behind Don Quixote springs from the truth that, in their respective ways, both visionaries made us see how perilously "iron" their Iron Ages are.

Notes

Note: All references in this essay to the text of *Etruscan Places* are from *D. H. Lawrence and Italy* (New York: Viking Press, 1972).

1. Harry T. Moore, *The Priest of Love*, (New York: Farrar, Straus & Giroux, 1974), pp. 429-30.
2. Christopher Hassall, "D. H. Lawrence and the Etruscans," *Essays by Divers Hands* 31 (1962): 71. See also Tom Morris's *"On Etruscan Places" (Paunch* (April, 1975): 8-39) which concentrates on Etruscan art and architecture and Lawrence's responses to them, as well as on Fascist Italy in 1927 and Lawrence's reaction to it, and Del Ivan Janik's *"Etruscan Places*: the Mystery of Touch," *Essays in Literature*, vol. 3 (1976): 194-205. L. D. Clark has a long book-manuscript that was recently accepted for publication, which deals with the symbolism of travel throughout Lawrence's writings, including substantial sections on all four travel books.)
3. Ibid., p. 77.
4. R. E. Pritchard, *D. H. Lawrence: Body of Darkness*, (Pittsburgh, Penn.: University of Pittsburgh Press, 1971), 204-05.
5. Harry T. Moore, *Poste Restante: a Lawrence Travel Calendar* (Berkeley, Calif.: University of California Press, 1956), pp. 3-4.

D. H. Lawrence's Golden Age 115

6. Edward Nehls, *D. H. Lawrence: a Composite Biography* (Madison, Wis.: University of Wisconsin Press, 1959), III, 146.
7. Ibid., III, 160.
8. Raymond Bloch, *Ancient Civilizations of the Etruscans* (New York: Cowles Book Co., 1969), p. 9. See also Massimo Pallotino, *The Etruscans* (Harmondsworth, England: Penguin Books, 1955), ch. 2, "The Problem of Etruscan Origins."
9. W. K. C. Guthrie, *The Greeks and Their Gods* (Boston: Beacon Press, 1950), p. 136.
10. Bertrand Russell, *The History of Western Philosophy* (New York: Simon and Schuster, 1945), p. 44.
11. Theodor Mommsen, *The History of Rome* (Glencoe, Illinois: Free Press [n.d.]), vol. I, p. 160.
12. Charles Seltman, *Women in Antiquity* (London: Pan Books, 1956), p. 76.
13. Sibylle von Cles-Reden, *The Buried People: A Study of the Etruscan World* (London: Hart-Davis, 1955), p. 206.
14. Alain Hus, *The Etruscans* (New York: Grove Press, 1961), p. 162.
15. Pallotino, *The Etruscans*, pp. 151-52. See also p. 216.
16. Hugh Hencken, *Tarquinia and Etruscan Origins* (New York: Praeger, 1968), p. 26.
17. Ibid., p. 17.
18. Lawrence at times wanted to offer quantity as well in *Etruscan Places*. In an October 1927 letter to Alfred Knopf, he says he "intended to do twelve sketches in different places—but when I was ill, I left off at Volterra. . .if you felt at all keen about the Etruscan book, I'd sweat around Arezzo and Ciusi and Orvieto and those places, and do the other six sketches this autumn. But if you feel cool about it, then none of us need bother. . . .[I] don't feel up to much." (*Collected Letters*, 1009-10). Either Knopf continuing to feel "cool" about Lawrence's further "Etruscanizing," or Lawrence continuing to feel ill (he says in a letter to Catherine Carswell on January 8, 1928, that he has "been down and out this last six months"—*Collected Letters*, p. 1033), or both, have unfortunately deprived us of more Lawrence essays on the Etruscans. By July 1928, he was hoping to get back to Italy and "finish my Etruscans" (*Collected Letters*, p. 1069).
19. George Dennis, *The Cities and Cemeteries of Etruria* (London: John Murray, 1883), p. li.
20. Ibid., p. lxii.
21. Ibid., p. lxii.
22. D. H. Lawrence, *The Collected Letters of D. H. Lawrence*, ed. by Harry T. Moore (New York: Viking Press, 1962), pp. 925, 967.
23. Cles-Reden, *The Buried People*, p. 76.
24. D. H. Lawrence, *Fantasia of the Unconscious* (New York: Viking Press, 1960), p. 54.
25. Ibid., p. 55.
26. D. H. Lawrence, *Apocalypse* (New York: Viking Press, 1960), pp. 76-77.
27. Pallotino, *The Etruscans*, p. 168.
28. Ibid., p. 141.
29. Emeline Richardson, *The Etruscans: Their Art and Civilization* (Chicago: University of Chicago Press, 1964), p. 7.

30. Luisa Barti, *Etruscan Cities and Their Cultures* (Berkeley, Calif.: University of California Press, 1973), p. 209.
31. Pallotino, *The Etruscans*, p. 130.
32. Henri Frankfurt, et. al., *Before Philosophy: The Intellectual Adventure of Ancient Man* (Harmondworth, England: Penguin, 1949), p. 12. I am indebted to Sandra Gilbert (*Act of Attention*, p. 309n) for her reference to Frankfurt.
33. Frankfurt, *Before Philosophy*, p. 49.
34. Ibid., p. 11.
35. Ibid., p. 14.
36. Kenneth Inniss, *Lawrence's Bestiary* (The Hague: Mouton, 1971), p. 190.
37. Karl Mannheim, *Ideology and Utopia* (New York: Harcourt, Brace, and World, 1964), p. 134.
38. Pallotino, *The Etruscans* pp. 74-75. Cf. p. 84 ("Etruscan expansion...must have been so powerful...that it was able to achieve a political, territorial, and linguisitic unity...over most of...Italy...." Pallotino also asserts that the cultural influence of Etruria spread north of Italy.)
39. The power passage is deceptive moreover because, as Tom Morris observes, Lawrence, in dealing with the Etruscans, "seems to side-track the issue of political power by concentrating on the fact of 'truth' embodied within the Lucumo. He seems to be saying that *truth* makes *power* either irrelevant or at least of minor importance" ("On *Etruscan Places*" p. 23).
40. D. H. Lawrence, *Phoenix: the Posthumous Papers of D. H. Lawrence*, (New York: Viking Press, 1972), p. 290.
41. Kenneth Rexroth, *An Autobiographical Novel* (Garden City, New York: Doubleday, 1966), p. v.
42. D. H. Lawrence, *Selected Essays* (Harmondsworth, England: Penguin, 1950), p. 76.
43. D. H. Lawrence, *Women in Love* (New York: Viking Press, 1960), pp. 96-97.
44. E. W. Tedlock, Jr., *D. H. Lawrence and Sons and Lovers: Sources and Criticisms* (New York: N.Y.U. Press, 1965), p. 138.
45. Tom Morris in "On *Etruscan Places*" makes a point in some respects almost identical: "...inherent in the tolerated *social power* of the Lucomo is the ugly power and counterfeit knowledge of Il Duce" (p. 24).
46. Hus, *The Etruscans*, pp. 183, 186. See also Pallotino, *The Etruscans*, p. 167.
47. D. Randall-MacIver, *The Etruscans* (Oxford, Oxford University Press, 1927), p. 62.
48. D. H. Lawrence, *Selected Essays*, p. 287.
49. D. H. Lawrence, *Lady Chatterley's Lover* (New York: Bantam Books, 1968), p. 301.
50. Ibid., pp. 302-3.
51. Ibid., p. 349.
52. Jacques Heurgon, *Daily Life of the Etruscans* (London, Weidenfeld and Nicolson, 1964), pp. 58, 59.
53. Massimo Pallotino, *Art of the Etruscans* (New York: Vanguard, 1955, p. 21.
54. Raymond Bloch, *The Etruscans* (New York: Praeger, 1958), pp. 146-47.
55. H. H. Scullard, *The Etruscan Cities and Rome* (New York: Viking Press, 1967) p. 14.

56. Ibid., p. 52.
57. A different response can be found in Emeline Richardson's *The Etruscans: Their Art and Civilization*"... the reader will believe anything Lawrence says about ancient Etruria and the Etruscans only at his own risk" (p. 11).
58. Mark Spilka in *The Love Ethic of D. H. Lawrence* (Bloomington, Indiana: Indiana University Press, 1955), p. 41, makes some telling points against defining Lawrence as a Symbolist: "... the French *Symbolistes* were searching for the spiritual infinite, and Lawrence was not; his symbols operate at a different level of language than theirs, and for different ends; they are not suggestive evocations of timeless spiritual reality, but material and focal expressions of those vague but powerful forces of nature which occur, quite patiently, in time." Among critics who regard Lawrence as a Symbolist are William York Tindall (*The Later D. H. Lawrence*) and R. P. Pritchard ("The aesthetic," says Professor Pritchard, commenting on one of the Tarquinia chapters, "is not one of superficial casualness but derives from a Symbolist aesthetic of *correspondence*, and intuition..."--*D. H. Lawrence: Body of Darkness*, p. 202)
59. Lionel Trilling, *Sincerity and Authenticity* (Cambridge, Mass.: Harvard University Press, 1972), p. 92.
60. Baruch Hochman, *Another Ego: The Changing View of Self and Society in the Work of D. H. Lawrence* (Columbia, S.C.: University of South Carolina Press, 1970), p. 261.
61. *Culture and Society, 1780-1950* (Garden City, New York: Anchor Books, 1960), p. 228.
62. Miguel Cervantes, *Don Quixote* (New York: New American Library, 1964), pp. 117-18.

5

Circles and Arcs: The Rhythm of Circularity and Centrifugality in *Last Poems*

People generally think that there are only two "last poems" by D. H. Lawrence: "Bavarian Gentians" and "The Ship of Death." A casual inspection of the sixty-seven poems in the Pinto-Roberts edition of *The Complete Poems of D. H. Lawrence* seems at first to bear out this impression; one tires of Lawrence's point-blank tendentiousness and exhortation in poems like "Demiurge," "The Breath of Life," "The Four," "Evil is Homeless," and others. In many of these last poems, Lawrence seems to violate almost all the rules of poetics set down by New Critics: mirror tricks with "personae," autotelism, no authorial insistence, a paradox or two, and a good dose of irony. Indeed some of the poems in *Last Poems* are marred by a talkative intensity, a somewhat oppressive eschatological solemnity and a fragmentariness not entirely absolved by thematic dovetailing between poems.

The guiding idea to keep in mind is that many of the poems in Lawrence's *Last Poems* cohere as a larger artistic design through a pattern of figurative centrifugality and circularity. These conceptual constructs denote, respectively, a movement outward from a center and an endless movement around a center. Applied to human experience and sensibility, centrifugality can be taken to connote selflessness, and circularity selfishness. How does this theoretical material inform these poems thematically? Modern people can choose between a mechanistic self-centeredness ("circularity") and an identification or integration with the living forces of the universe ("centrifugality"). This controlling thematic opposition can be illustrated first by citing and briefly explaining instances of "centrifugality" and "circularity" in the poems. "All that matters is to be at one with the living god" ("Pax," p. 700). With the Christian metaphorical convention of "rising" to God in mind, one can discern in "being at one" with God a centrifugal movement of a human being upwards, away from the average self and the general human condition.

> Oh, do not tell me the heavens as well are
> a wheel.
> For every revolution of the earth around
> the sun
> is a footstep onwards, onwards, we know
> not whither. . . .
>
> For life is a wandering, we know not whither,
> but going.
>
> Only the wheel goes around, but it never wanders.
> It stays on its hub.
> ("The Wandering Cosmos," p. 713)

This quotation contains both a centrifugal and a circular figure. The first four lines cited describe a centrifugal movement in its emphasis on "a footstep onwards, onwards," suggesting both the modern astronomical theory of an expanding universe, and a noncircular progression ("wandering"), which, as the poem informs us, describes the essential movement of sun, earth, and life. The last two lines indicate circularity, and, significantly, present this motion as a wheel, a basic mechanism and mechanistic conception.

> And it is time to go, to bid farewell
> to one's own self. . .
> . . .
> For the voyage of oblivion awaits you.
> ("The Ship of Death," pp. 716, 720)

The movement away from one's conscious self toward oblivion (whether psychic transformation or physical death) describes a departure from "I" consciousness as a centrifugal activity.

And still through knowledge and will . . .
man can break away, and fall from the
   hands of God
into himself alone . . .
a god-lost creature turning upon himself
                              ("Abysmal Immortality," p. 700)

"Turning upon himself" and "revolving upon himself" identify the punishment of excessive cerebrality and willfulness as an egoistic circularity.

And men that sit in machines
among spinning wheels, in an apotheosis
   of wheels
sit in the grey mist of movement which
   moves not
and going which goes not
and doing which does not
and being which is not. . . .
                          ("Evil is Homeless," p. 711)

Circularity and mechanization are once again united as a figurative and thematic statement of the entrapment of industrialized man. In addition, four statements of paradoxical movement and nonmovement depict the phenomenon of circularity as well as Lawrence's conception of evil (which is anything not coordinated with the centrifugal universe, and "thus" unnatural).

Only the human being, absolved from kissing
   and strife
goes on and on and on, without wandering
fixed upon the hub of the ego
going, yet never wandering, fixed, yet in
   motion,
. . .

And thou shalt begin to spin round on the
  hub of the obscene ego . . .
     ("Death Is Not Evil, Evil Is Mechanical," p.713)

This example implies another thematic form of centrifugality, the "kissing and strife" that Lawrence felt to be integral to a passionate and vital relationship. The human being "absolved from kissing and strife" is doomed to the paradox of fixed motion, "spinning" on his ego.

One can find instances in *Last Poems* that diverge from this pattern of "evil" circularity and "good" centrifugality, such as these vaguely centripetal lines from "Song of Death": "for the cosmos even in death is like a dark whorled shell / whose whorls fold round to the core of soundless silence and pivotal oblivion / where the soul comes at last, and has utter peace." (p. 724) But poems of "positive" centripetality and circularity are outnumbered by poems indicating a movement from one's personality toward a merging into the universe. In philosophic terms, Lawrence's dying man (Lawrence himself and the reader) transcends the dualistic subject-object dichotomy that the English Romantic poets tussled with continuously in their quasi-identification with the natural environment.

One may also formulate centrifugality as a sense of movement between opposites, a vitalist tension reminiscent of Blake. This trope spins through "Death Is Not Evil, Evil Is Mechanical":

Know thyself, and that thou are mortal.
But know thyself, denying that thou are mortal:
a thing of kisses and strife
a lit-up shaft of rain
a calling column of blood
a rose tree bronzey with thorns
a mixture of yea and nay
a rainbow of love and hate
a wind that blows back and forth
a creature of beautiful peace, like a river
and a creature of conflict, like a cataract:
know thyself, in denial of all these things—

And thou shall begin to spin round on the
   hub of
the obscene ego.
(p. 714)

The contrastive placement of the circular reference in the last line accentuates all the preceding centrifugal imagery in the poem.

A scrutiny of diction will support the idea also suggested by thematic overlapping that some of the poems in this collection form a network. One discerns a diction of rigidity, sterility, and life-in-death in six consecutive poems ("Evil is Homeless," "What Then is Evil?," "The Evil World-Soul," "The Wandering Cosmos," "Death is Not Evil, Evil is Mechanical," and "Strife"): "grey," "machines," "wheels," "iron," "absolute," "absolution," "absolute consciousness," "Neutrality," "hub," "fixed," "ego," "void," "centre," "Robot," and "round." Four of these words are also circular images, and such words as "machines," "ego," and "Robot" connote the circularity of mechanical and obsessive processes.

Themes crystallizing around this diction can be conceptually sorted out as follows: modernity, mechanization, egoism, will as an absolute, paralysis as a centering stillness (a paradoxical mobility-and-immobility the opposite of Eliot's quasi-mystical "still point of the turning world" in "Burnt Norton"). All these themes converge and culminate in the theme of the World War in the three poems immediately following "Strife": "The Late War," "Murder" (which by its subject and its position between "The Late War" and "Murderous Weapons" implies the war), and "Murderous Weapons," and in the last poem of this group, "Departure," in which the war is the objectification of an "evil world soul," a world where "wheels are evil and machines are evil." In "Evil is Homeless," modern industrial experience is likened to a homeless, skulking ("grey hyena") existence separated from the august polarities of heaven and Lawrence's Persephonic hell. Our experience has become a mechanistic movement that goes nowhere, does nothing, is nothing, but which like Blake's "Satanic Mills" encompasses all. In the next poem, "What Then Is Evil?" (and the "then" can be regarded as a sign of intended linkage among these poems), the wheel is spotlighted as a metaphor of lifelessness, of energy that represents death or death-in-life because it is doomed to revolve eternally. An analogy is established between the inhumanly rigid individual will and the inflexible wheel-based mechanization of industry and technology to suggest that modern man and society, rather than progressing toward and creating fresh experiences, are both caught up in a perpetual self-obsession and sterility of social modes.

The master metaphor unifying this cluster of diction in the poems from "Evil is Homeless" to "Departure" is circularity. Such a figurative self-centering of the mechanized, mechanizing will violates all sense and possibility of phase, process, and journey, and symbolizes the barrenness of our age on corresponding individual and public levels. A definition of obscenity in the poem "Death is Not Evil" expands the theme of the perils of ego-obsession, a self-absorption that like masturbation does not engage the "Other," the kisses and strife," of life's natural pulsations and counter-rhythms.

If a number of the poems can be considered overtly anticircular (such as "What Then Is Evil?" and "The Evil World Soul"), others are overtly centrifugal. "The Wandering Cosmos" denies that the movement of the universe itself is a wheel-like circularity, insisting on a curvilinear outward progression ("For every revolution of the earth around the sun is a footstep onwards. . . . . .a step onwards in untravelled space"), so that man and his universe merge in a trajectory through new space and new experience. Ideas of change as part of a basic rhythm of life instance centrifugality once again, for, as Lawrence puts it in "Kissing and Horrid Strife," man, by virtue of inevitable vulnerability to the "angels" and the "Sunderers," most keenly experiences possibilities for fulfillment through a contact with some other person or force that moves him out of the "deadly center." In this sense even the Heaven and Hell of "When Satan Fell" establish polarities needed for the oscillations man must experience if, as Lawrence sees it, he is to avoid the gray centripetal nullity of an ego-centered life. As the next poem, "Doors," states, "... evil is a third thing. ... in another place," not the Plutonic underworld of this poem, and, in a grander setting, of "Bavarian Gentians."

The last form of centrifugality as a rhythmic phase or outward movement is located in the "oblivion" poems. These include virtually all seventeen poems after "The Ship of Death," and, together with that major poem, depict Lawrence's posture toward approaching death.[1] Poignant in their intensely personal character, not all of these poems are especially good, but all are imbued with a serenity and quietness striking in the usually throbbing Lawrence. Death is not euphemized or glamorized; as the title of "Difficult Death" points up, oblivion is a "bitter passage." In the next poem "All Souls' Day," we are told to be careful and gentle about death, "For it is hard to die," and the title of this poem clearly universalizes the applicability of this event, as well as designating its religious quality. Terms like "journey" in this and in many of the "oblivion" poems indicate the centrifugality metaphor of death as a passage from our known self into "... a darkness invisible enfolded in the deeper dark."

> For the soul has a long, long journey
>   after death
> to the sweet home of pure oblivion.
>   ("All Souls' Day," p. 721)

> the little slender soul sits swiftly down,
>   and takes the oars
> and draws away, away, towards dark depths
>   ("After All Saints' Day," p. 723)

> So build your ship of death, and let the

soul
drift to dark oblivion.
                  ("Difficult Death," p. 721)

    Death as a journey is hardly a new metaphor (going back to those pre-Hellenic-star-worshipping cultures that Lawrence admired so greatly in his *Apocalypse*), but it provided Lawrence with a conventionalized medium within which to make death more bearable by presenting it as a condition of humanity experienced by all, while simultaneously underlining its distinctively individual nature. Death becomes another form of movement away from ourselves, a centrifugal descent. Obliteration of one's self is perhaps what makes death most alarming to contemplate. It indicates therefore a remarkable coherence in Lawrence's writings that his manner of accepting death as a ritual voyage can also be identified with his ideology of "blood-consciousness" in the abandoment of cerebral egoism; those instinctive and intuitive energies that Lawrence felt gave depth and integrity to life also carry one most naturally through death.[2] In identifying himself with the "deep oblivion of earth's lapse and renewal" ("Shadows"), in passing through the "waters of oblivion" ("Change"), in being able to forget "once dipped in dark oblivion" ("The End, the Beginning"), one achieves "inward and lovely peace" and yield[s]/ to God who dwells in deep oblivion" ("Forget"). This temerity toward death gives a compelling tonal authority to poems some might fault for insufficient semantic indirection or linguistic vibration.

    Some of the poems also suggest a "return" trip, and thus produce a rewarding ambiguity about the nature of death. This motif appears in several poems of the "oblivion" group, but most majestically in "The Ship of Death," possibly the prime centrifugal poem in the collection. For if any poem in *Last Poems* describes a rite, this one does, and all the more poignantly for reevoking the death ritual of the ancient Egyptians while simultaneously and thus ironically describing an age in which people do not know how to confront death. The "longest journey" patently indicates a centrifugal dimension in the "oblivion" poems, but in "Ship" itself the journey occupies only the last one-third of the poem. The poem nevertheless opens with three centrifugal references:

Now it is autumn and the falling fruit
and the long journey towards oblivion.
                        (ll. 1-2)

The apples falling . . .
to bruise themselves an exit from themselves.
                        (ll. 3-4)

And it is time to go, to bid farewell
to one's own self, and find an exit
    from the fallen self.
                        (ll. 5-7)

These references, by linking the season of decline in nature and a mythic (and declining) fruit with fallen and declining mankind, establish a universal condition of inexorable deterioration within both a naturalistic and a religious context.

The first half of "Ship" concerns preparation; the season anticipating death, late autumn, is described, and the style of the death is stressed, focusing on the archaic, Hamletic "quietus," which enobles us with its tragic reference and rules out violent, unnatural death. One must be spiritually ready for death, attuned to the "season" and to an acceptance of one's naturally decrepit self (". . . our bodies fallen, bruised, badly bruised"), and yet realize that this "journey" is a "long and painful death." The journey in "our" little ship—with its ("our") little food, little cakes and wine—finally begins. It appears at first to be circular ("There is no port, there is nowhere to go"), but the use of darkness to create a process of ego-dissolution as well as an obliteration of life describes a symbolic centrifugality, paradoxically climaxed in the line "and the little ship is there; yet she is gone." If this were a circular experience, the little ship would still be "there."

> There is no port, there is nowhere to go
> only the deepening blackness darkening still
> blacker upon the soundless, ungurgling flood
> darkness at one with darkness, up and down
> and sideways utterly dark, so there is no
>   direction any more
> and the little ship is there; yet she is
>   gone.
> She is not seen for there is nothing to see
>   her by.
> She is gone! gone! and yet
> somewhere she is there.
> Nowhere!

Although Tom Brangwen's death in "The Marsh and the Flood" chapter of *The Rainbow* depicts a real drowning in all its terror, the marked imagistic similarity between the passage in the novel and that in "The Ship of Death" just quoted underscores the gravity of this "journey," despite any ambiguities about the nature of the death.

The metaphor of centrifugality in this poem then presents a movement from consciousness as egoism to unconsciousness as oblivion through the journey into "blackness," but it also assumes the appearance of a journey from life to biological death. Any indication of biological death is minimized, however, by the hint of a return in sections nine and ten, in one of the most moving passages in modern poetry:

> The flood subsides, and the body, like a
>   worn seashell
> emerges strange and lovely.
> And the little ship wings home, faltering
>   and lapsing
> on the pink flood,
> and the frail soul steps out, into her
>   house again
> filling the heart with peace.

That return suggests more of symbolic than a physical death, the birth of a new sensibility transcending a former hyperconscious self. A vague life-after-life mysticism also operates here.[3] But more important, one beholds in "The Ship of Death" a bold affirmative example of the centrifugal lunge towards the most fearful unknown. The capacity of the metaphor to include even the extremity of approaching death indicates that Lawrence established in *Last Poems* a counterpoise of death-in-life and the integrated life that is finally art.

Notes

1. Sandra Gilbert, *Acts of Attention: The Poems of D. H. Lawrence* (Ithaca, New York: Cornell University Press, 1972). "Here [in "The Ship of Death"] for the first time Lawrence becomes absolutely explicit about his own death and the death that man is dying during every moment of his life" (p. 307). See also Tom Marshall, *The Psychic Mariner: A Reading of the Poems of D. H. Lawrence* (New York: Viking Press, 1970). "'The Ship of Death' is the culmination of the theme of death and resurrection in Lawrence's whole work" (p. 215).

2. Elizabeth Cipolla, "The 'Last Poems' of D. H. Lawrence," *The D. H. Lawrence Review*, vol. 2, no. 2 (Summer, 1969) makes a relevant point about the relation of life and death in *Last Poems:* "Lawrence felt himself to be on the verge of the last great revelation, the knowledge that life and death and rebirth are one in an unfathomable mystery of being" (p. 118).

3. Michael Kirham, "D. H. Lawrence's *Last Poems*" *The D. H. Lawrence Review*, vol. 5, no. 2 (Summer, 1972): 197-220, perceives another aspect of immortality suggested by *Last Poems* as a whole: the "thought movement" of *Last Poems* is toward "the construction of a state of mind that will steady him [Lawrence] in the face of death, 'survive' death in that sense" (p. 102).

6

"A New Heaven and an Old Earth:" Lawrence's *Apocalypse*, Apocalyptic, and the *Book of Revelation*

"What we care about is the release of the imagination. . . . What does the Apocalypse matter, unless in so far as it give us imaginative release into another vital world?" (D. H. Lawrence, *Phoenix*)

"The end is where we start from." (T. S. Eliot, "Little Gidding")

" . . .the real birth is the second birth." (Norman O. Brown, *Love's Body*)

"No one can speak for liberty without passing through revolution to apocalypse" (Milton, *Areopagatica*).

"The eschatological attitude is by no means alien to our times." (Kenneth Burke, Preface to Austin Farrar's *A Rebirth of Images: The Making of St. John's Apocalypse*).

". . .for the time is at hand" (*Revelation*, Ch. 22, v. 13).

I

"The Revelation of St. John," said D. H. Lawrence late in life, "is a book to conjure with." Lawrence's *Apocalypse* is the last full-length prose writing of his career, and virtually his last chance to "conjure." Although praised by a few, *Apocalypse* seems generally to be known only for a few famous passages, such as Lawrence's eulogy of the horse in the ancient world, and the paean to life in the concluding pages.[1] But the book deserves more attention than this, in part because it attempts a whole-scale interpretation of the most enigmatic and disturbing book in the Bible. The iconoclastic nature of Lawrence's interpretation poses further complications for a critic of his venture. For in Lawrence's *Apocalypse*, as, he insisted, within *Revelation*, another world of thought and values obtains. My plan in this chapter is to sort out a few major strains in both *Apocalypse* and *Revelation*, and to scrutinize them in the light of ideas about the two works, and about the subject of apocalyptic, offered by representative theologians, historians, revolutionists, and literary scholars. More specifically, I intend to examine *Apocalypse* as transvaluation, and for further material on Lawrence's conception of the "Old World" sensibility, an area containing a significant esthetic. I will also attempt to analyze both *Revelation* and *Apocalypse* for elitist ideas and concepts of power, cardinal elements in the two works given scant attention. Apocalypticism (or apocalyptic, to use the theological term) will also be discussed as psychic illness, eschatology, revolution, and as a symptom of human plight. I will consider the presence of antianthropomorphic elements in *Apocalypse*, which can be regarded as a libertarian vein in Lawrence's scheme of values, and conclude with a discussion of the antiapocalyptic in his last book, a motif stemming from Lawrence's iconoclasm, and closely related to his vitalism.

I wish to indicate immediately that I am not embarking on a comprehensive or thorough exegesis of either Saint John's or Lawrence's Apocalypse. My goal will be less to show whether Lawrence was "right" in his thesis that *Revelation* is a disguised or transformed version of an older "pagan" myth, than to discern what sort of vision of human sensibility and polity issues from his transvaluative interpretation of the culminating book of *The New Testament*.[2]

I will first present a few general interpretations and evaluations of *Revelation* by reputed *Revelation* scholars in order to establish a foil for Lawrence's conttribution to the field. According to Austin Farrar, a Doctor of Divinity at Trinity College, Oxford, *Revelation* "is the one great poem which the first Christian age produced, it is a single and living unity from end to end, it contains a whole world of spiritual imagery to be entered into and possessed."[3] Dr. Farrar acknowledges borrowings evident in *Revelation*, but asserts that they "no more disfigure his work than Virgil's or Milton's disfigure theirs" (pp. 6-7). Lawrence, conversely, insists that Saint John the Divine not only borrowed from, or perhaps unconsciously transmitted, older religious sources, but that he partly transformed them into a Judeo-Christian ideological allegory.

R. H. Charles, a former Archdeacon of Canterbury and a towering figure in *Revelation* scholarship, author of a large two-volume commentary on *Revelation* that Lawrence had read, also cites a point about these borrowings: "There are certain statements and doctrines in the Apocalypse which could not have been written first-hand by a Christian. These are in some cases of Jewish origin, but others are ultimately derived from Babylonian, Egyptian, or Greek sources."[4] Charles describes a central trait of *Revelation* as a form of apocalyptic: "Apocalyptic is a philosophy of history and religion. . . . It takes within its purview not only the present and the last things, but all things past, present, and to come" (p. clxxxvi). By this account, *Revelation* is not only eschatology, but a vast moral cosmology. "Apocalyptic and not Greek philosophy," adds Charles, "was the first to grasp the great idea that all history, alike human, cosmological, and spiritual, is a unity—a unity following naturally as a corollary of the unity of God" (p. clxxxvi).

Lawrence himself gives a concise description of *Revelation* from the traditional perspective:

. . . what meaning *has* the Apocalypse?. . . . it means a prophetic vision of the martyrdom of the Christian Church, the Second Advent, the destruction of worldly power, particularly the power of the great Roman Empire, and then the institution of the Millenium, the rule of the risen Martyrs of Christendom for the space of one thousand years; after which, the end of everything, the Last Judgment, and souls in heaven; all earth, moon and sun being wiped out, all stars and all space. The New Jerusalem, and Finis!

This.... is the orthodox interpretation of the Apocalypse, and probably it is the true superficial meaning, or final intentional meaning of the work.[5]

"But what of it," concludes Lawrence bluntly, "It is a bore."

If Farrar and Charles provide sophisticated conceptions of *Revelation* as artistic and religious visions respectively, the *Revelation* scholar Hubert J. Richards offers a profound construction of a different order: " . . . a deeper analysis of the book indicates that its message is the entirely new one—that victory is so near that it has arrived. The death and resurrection of Christ is valid for all time, because it is a victory which is irreversible, and therefore always present. And the Church's victory is constantly being achieved . . . not only in spite of persecution but because of it. . . . The opposition he [the persecuted Christian] experiences from the world, and his struggle with it, is his victory."[6] Dr. Richards adds that the "central theme of *Revelation* is timeless, and not tied down to any particular historic period" (p. 20).

Frank Kermode regards *Revelation* as a fundamental type of the theory of fictions, a means used by man to evade or transcend death by joining the beginning and the end: "I begin by discussing fictions of the End—about ways in which, under varying existential pressures, we have imagined the ends of the world. This . . . will provide clues to the ways in which fictions, whose ends are consonant with origins, and in concord, however unexpected, with their precedents, satisfy our needs. So we begin with Apocalypse, which ends, transforms, and is concordant."[7]

To avoid being confounded by the heady character of *Revelation*, with its messianic violence and idealism, one might enlist Professor John R. May's humanizing and sobering rationale in his study of apocalyptic in the American novel: "... the precise raison d'etre for apocalyptic is to deny the imminence of easy victory, to force Jews and Christians alike to accept the agony of history, the birth-pangs of creation."[8] (What Kermode calls "clerkly scepticism" denies imminence altogether as an expectation (in life or in art), or, rather, drives it within, converting imminence to immanence.[9]) One could question, though, as Lawrence does, whether apocalyptic really makes certain kinds of people accept history (and all that such acceptance implies), or goads them to pounce on it with all the more history-denying faith at the evolution of the next eschatological *saeculum* (such as the year 1000—or 2000).

II

Thus *Revelation* (and apocalyptic) is a crisis theology, a vision of catastrophic suffering for the evildoers (who of course vary from one apocalyptical period to another) as retribution for the suffering wreaked upon the faithful. As we are told in *Revelation*, the wicked "shall have their part in the lake which burneth with fire and brimstone" (Rev. 21:8) whereas the holy, according to John, shall inherit "a new heaven and a new earth" (21:1), the holy city "coming down from God out of heaven" (21:2), for "the tabernacle of God *is* with men, and he will dwell with them ..." (21:3). Thus by the terms of this apocalypse, the good shall enjoy a second and eternal life, and the evil (at that time, the Emperor Domitian—though regarded by some as Nero—and the Roman Empire) a second and eternal death.

A few words about the historical period in which *Revelation* was written might further clarify certain fundamental attitudes permeating *Revelation*. According to *Harper's Biblical Dictionary*, "The enforcement of emperor worship in the latter part of the reign of Domitian, A.D. 81-96, threatened the Christians of Asia Minor with a dangerous crisis. The author

[Saint John] believed that universal persecution was about to break on the church."[10] *Revelation* itself excitingly conveys something of the momentous atmosphere of the times, that essentially apocalyptic sense of cosmic immimence: " . . . the great day of his wrath is come; and who shall be able to stand?" (6:17), "the time is at hand," (1:3), and "I John, who also am your brother, and companion in tribulation, and in the kingdom and patience of Jesus Christ . . . " (1:9). One thinks of other large "imminent" moments, religious or secular, such as Lenin "at the Finland Station," the pause before the epoch-creating activization (for better or worse) of a new human vision of man and society, a sense in the air that God or History is about to intervene in human affairs, and that all past misery and injustice will shortly be vindicated eternally for all the faithful and downtrodden.

If Lawrence thought (as we shall see later) that apocalyptical ideology and *Revelation* bore destructive, even nihilistic, properties, so have others. Along these lines perhaps the most famous work in English in our time is Norman Cohn's *The Pursuit of the Millenium*, a study of messianic personnages, movements, and ideas throughout Western Christian civilization. Professor Cohn regards the vision of *Daniel*, written around 165 B.C., as "the paradigm of what was to become and to remain the central phantasy of revolutionary eschatology. The world is dominated by an evil, tyrannous power of boundless destructiveness—a power moreover that is imagined not as simply human but as demonic. The tyranny of that power will become more and more outrageous, the sufferings of its victims more and more intolerable—until suddenly the hour will strike when the Saints of God are able to rise up and overthrow it. Then the Saints themselves . . . shall in their turn inherit dominion over the whole earth. This will be the culmination of history . . . "[11]

Cohn then discusses messianic revolutionary movements in broad terms that could include *Revelation* and the social and religious culture behind it:

... amongst the masses in the over-populated, highly urbanized areas there were always many who lived in a state of chronic and inescapable insecurity, harassed not only by their economic helplessness and vulnerability but by the lack of . . . traditionial social relationshps. . . . These were the people whose anxieties drove them to seek messianic leaders and they were also the people who were most prone to create demonic scapegoats. The resulting paranoid phantasy could easily be integrated into the old eschatology dervied from the Johannine and Sibylline traditions. In this form it became a coherent social myth which was capable of taking entire possession of those who believed in it. It explained their suffering, it promised them recompense, it held their anxieties at bay, it gave them an illusion of security—even while it drove them . . . on a quest which was always vain and often suicidal.

So it came about that multitudes of people acted out with fierce energy a shared phantasy which . . . brought them such intense emotional relief that they could live only through it and were perfectly willing to die for it. It is a phenomenon which was to recur many times between the eleventh century and the sixteenth century, . . . which is not irrelevant to the growth of totalitarin movements, with their messianic leaders, their millenial mirages and their demon scapegoats, in the present century [Pp. 73-74].

Cohn's treatment of eschatological mass movements is little affected by the distinctively religious spirit of messianism, let alone apocalyptic. Though Cohn gives some attention to the desperate social conditions that have driven masses of people to the extremes of hope and despair implicit in apocalyptic faith, perhaps more attention and some empathy might have further humanized his portrayal and even transformed his attitude. Cohn's position epitomizes the sort of surgical conceptualization and condescension of the modern social sciences that leaves one feeling that the individual self has been utterly disregarded.

Friedrich Engels, on the other hand, manages to introduce a humanizing warmth and concreteness into Cohn's "masses":

What kind of people were the first Christians recruited from? Mainly from the 'laboring and burdened,' the members of the lowest strata of the people, as becomes a revolutionary element. And what did they consist of? In the towns of impoverished free men, . . . then of emancipated slaves, and, above all, actual slaves; on the large estates in Italy, Sicily, and Africa, of slaves, and in the rural districts of the provinces of small peasants who had fallen more and more into bondage through debt. There was absolutely no common road to emancipation for all these elements. For all of them paradise lay behind them; for the ruined free men it was the former *polis* . . . of which their forefathers had been free citizens; for the war-captive slaves, the time of freedom before their subjugation and captivity; for the small peasants, the abolished gentile social system and communal land ownership. All that had been smitten down by the leveling iron fist of conquering Rome. . . . Any resistance of isolated small tribes or towns to the gigantic Roman world power was hopeless. Where was the way out . . . common to all these groups of people whose interests were mutually alien or even opposed? And yet it had to be found if a great revolutionary movement was to embrace them all.[12]

Although Engels would possibly be accused by some of distorting the past in identifying a correspondence between the early apocalypticists and the secular revolutionary movements of nineteenth-century Europe, his perspective is certainly not stigmatized by the elitism and snobbery in Lawrence's interpretation of *Revelation*. And Cohn at least offers a motivation for the desperate beliefs and actions of apocalytpic movements.

Cohn extends his indictment from a social concept of mass behavior to one of individual psychosis: "The megalomaniacal view of oneself as the Elect, wholly good, abominably persecuted yet assured of ultimate triumph; the attribution of gigantic and demonic powers to the adversary; the refusal to accept the ineluctable limitations and imperfections of human existence, such as transience, dissension, conflict, fallibility whether intellectual or moral; the obsession with inerrable prophecies—these attitudes are symptoms of . . . paranoid."[13]

Despite the value of possessing a sense of "transience, dissension, conflict, fallibility," in any concern with human nature and societal organization, one wonders whether the function and worth of mass revolutionary movements can be so easily dismissed, despite their excesses, or even their consolidation (and betrayal) as totalitarianism. Their very rise bespeaks a deep need for coping with acute suffering deliberately imposed. Though Lawrence is far less libertarian than Cohn in spurning the Judeo-Christian vision of an eschatological Elect composed of the very people hammered into the ground by the secular authorities, both men seem insensitive to the horrible fact that life under certain conditions could at most be made bearable only by fantasies or visions of cataclysmic change.

III

Lawrence, however, spurns not only the Elect of *Revelation*, but *Revelation* itself. This rejection constitutes one of the crowning ironies of his own revelation. *Apocalypse*, besides containing a testamentary vision of the nature of the Good Life, harbors a formidable denunciation and transvaluational reading of *Revelation*. To examine *Apocalypse* as either transvaluation or denunciation, we must first realize Lawrence's profound need to find a body of thought or doctrine in antiquity (or anywhere else) that would lend objective verification to his own. Frederick Carter, for whose book *The Dragon of the Apocalypse* Lawrence's own *Apocalypse* was originally designed as an introductory essay, implies that the search for doctrinal "correspondences" could result in an iconoclastic approach to *Revelation*:

> Somewhere in paganism, he [Lawrence] maintained steadily, must exist a document definitive of its ancient way of

thought and of its process. Explanation must be yet extant, giving the firm principles whereby they envisaged and absorbed the universe in whole and through which they attained the dark power to penetrate in thought to that underworld which is below our conscious level now. Man, he asserted, then mastered things not by thought of the conscious kind only, or so much, as by the thrust of the underconscious will and desire in him.[14]

Carter's interpretation can be readily assimilated to the metaphysic informing Lawrence's work generally, but it also suggests Lawrence's proclivity to "conjure." What one could ask is whether Lawrence's conjuration about *Revelation* leads to an objectively accurate depiction, or, something not necessarily inferior, an imaginatively viable recreation, of the ancient, non-Hellenic mind.

Eugene Goodheart in *The Utopian Vision of D. H. Lawrence* has pointed out that "Lawrence performed the remarkable feat of preserving in his imagination the precognitive sense of the mythical mind: the sense that all the bodies of the world, animate and inanimate, are living sacred selves bound to each other in a mysterious, incomprehensible flow."[15] Professor Goodheart's hylozoistic formulation offers a useful approach to Lawrence's work concerned with "Old-World" thinking.[16] It is best to deal with this area by looking into Lawrence's ideas about the "physiology of consciousness," for these two sections of his theorizing are basically unified.

Lawrence harbored (and borrowed) esoteric ideas about the human body in order to corroborate his own esthetic and metaphysical interests. More specifically, he had a conception of the structure of the psyche that reflected his well-known division of sensibility into "mental" and "blood" consciousness. Although he develops this idea more elaborately in *Fantasia of the Unconscious*, it is presented succinctly in the earlier *The Symbolic Meaning*, the first version of *Studies in Classic American Literature*.[17] The pertinence of this "physiology" to the idea of a precognitive mind is that in part it also embodies, according to Lawrence, the form and mode of operation of the ancient mind, particularly among the intellectuals of the time, the priestly caste:

> What we know as sensual consciousness has its fountain head in the plexus of the abdomen; what we know as spiritual consciousness has its issue in the cardiac plexus. . . .
> Our mental consciousness is a third thing, resultant from this duality in precerebral cognition. . . .
> This knowledge, . . . the psyche comprising our whole consciousness, physical, sensual, spiritual, precerebral as well as cerebral—seems to have been familiar to the pagan priesthoods and to the esoteric mystics of the past. We can only begin to understand the initiation into the religious mysteries . . . when we can grasp the rise of precerebral consciousness in the great plexuses, and the movement of passional or dynamic cognition from one centre to another, toward culmination or consummation in what we may call whole-experience, or whole-consciousness.
> It is quite certain that the preChristian priesthoods understood the processes of *dynamic* consciousness, which is a precerebral consciousness. It is certain that John gives us in the Apocalypse a cypher-account of the process of the conquest of the lower or sensual dynamic centres by the upper or spiritual dynamic consciousness, a conquest affected centre by centre, toward a culmination in the *actual* experience of spiritual infinitude. . . .
> This priestly knowledge, however, was inevitably sensual. The sensual understanding was the living field of the ancient world. The one-sidedness of exclusively sensual understanding caused the downfall of the old systems.[18]

In the analogy that Lawrence makes here between the Old World mind and our modern psychoanalytic concept of the unconscious, stress should be placed on his insistence that this ancient, precerebral consciousness is more impressive than either the Freudian or the Jungian psyche. The "unconscious" or "dynamic consciousness" of the ancients, Lawrence feels, is more positive in its influence upon "mental consciousness" than Freud's conception, and more "physical" than Jung's. *Revelation*, moreover, appears covertly to contain the esoteric process by which Christianity imprisoned visceral being for the sake of glorifying mental consciousness as spirituality, resulting, for Lawrence, in psychic fragmentation.

"Blood consciousness," in other words, is supposedly the mode and form of cerebration of the pre- or non-Hellenic people. That Lawrence is not only seeking justification of his own doctrine is implicit in his pointing out the "one-sidedness of *exclusively* [italics added] sensual knowledge" developing negative qualities, adding shortly after that "the sensual consciousness, hopelessly dominant, had become destructive and tyrannical in the human psyche" (p. 70).

One manifestation of this ancient consciousness, whether the result of intimacy of the mind with the great plexuses or not, was a relatedness to the natural environment so intense as to be qualitatively different from ours:

> Don't let us imagine we see the sun as the old civilisations saw it. All we see is a scientific little luminary, dwindled to a ball of blazing gas. In the centuries before Ezekiel and John, the sun was still a magnificent reality, men drew forth from him strength and splendour, and gave him back homage and lustre and thanks. But in us, the connection is broken, the responsive centres are dead. . . . We have lost the cosmos, by coming out of responsive connection with it, and this is our chief tragedy. What is our petty little love of nature—Nature!—compared to the ancient magnificent living with the cosmos. . . .
> [*Apocalypse*, pp. 41-42.]

This conception climaxes a few pages later in a organic figure of the human universe: "We and the cosmos are one. The cosmos is a vast living body, of which we are still parts. The sun is a great heart whose tremors run through our smallest veins. The moon is a great gleaming nerve-centre from which we quiver forever" (p. 45).

Implicit in this indivisibility between men and natural environment is an idea bearing highly significant social and cultural dimensions: " . . . the old Aegean culture is different from what we call Greek, especially in its religious basis. Every old civilisation . . . had a definitely religious basis. The nation was, in a very old sense, a church, or a vast cult-unit. From cult to culture is only a step, but took a lot of making. Cult-lore was the wisdom of the old races. We now have culture" (pp. 75-76). Goodheart has described this process in Lawrence's recreation of the Old World mind as a movement from logos to mythos. Critics hostile to Lawrence rather facilely subsume it under atavism or a cult of mindlessness, and, indeed, at its worst, it could somewhat resemble the modern tribalism of the *Volk*, or, less grimly, the Jesus-freak groups.[19]

A consequence of this organic interrelatedness of inner and outer is a character of mind that Lawrence prizes and tries to define:

> Man thought and still thinks in images. But now our images have hardly any emotional value. We always want a 'conclusion,' an end, we always want to come, in our mental processes, to a decision, a finality, a full stop. This gives us a sense of satisfaction. All our mental consciousness is a movement onwards, a movement in stages, like our sentences, and every full stop is a mile-stone that marks our 'progress' and our arrival somewhere. On and on we go, for the mental consciousness. Whereas of course there is no goal. Consciousness is an end in itself. We torture ourselves getting somewhere, and when we get there it is nowhere, for there is nowhere to get to.
> While men still thought of the heart or the liver as the seat of consciousness, they had no idea of this on-and-on-process of thought. To them a thought was . . . a cumulative thing, a deepening thing, in which feeling deepened into feeling in consciousness till there was a sense of fullness (*Apocalypse*, pp. 80-81).

Lawrence is intimating that this Old World thought is qualitative and "organic," rather than quantitative or "linear," like the modern mind. In the notion that "Consciousness is an end in itself," he also suggests two other matters: an antiapocalyptic attitude that has impressive implications, and an esthetic. It is strikingly ironic that an author so frequently accused of cultural barbarism should, of all the "fictions of the end" available, choose the one for his own End statement that his detractors accuse him of either lacking or rejecting: consciousness (and the context of the sentence, as of the passage in general, implies full development of consciousness, *high* consciousness). Lawrence, as Kermode observes, was a "clerkly writer, one too sophisticated to accept the naive promises of apocalyptic, yet, not unlike other sophisticated people, was also fascinated by it."[20] The polarizing of apocalyptic to a sense of history, verisimilitude, the here-and-now, created in Lawrence's better work an imaginative apparatus of enormous tensions and elasticities by which to measure the daily by the eternal, the moment (fleeting or consummate) by the eschatological, and vice-versa.

Lawrence utters a hard and brave truth when he says that we have nowhere to go, that there is no End, for his own mortal end was rising before him, perhaps with all the concrete immediacy and terror of the powerful "deepening black darkening still blacker" passage in "The Ship of Death." Also, in eliminating end, he is thinking in terms of "mythos" or "cult-thinking," and that represents a grave threat to our craving—"mental" or not—for pattern, order, the satisfaction surely biological as well a esthetic and emotional that we derive from interlacing our beginnings and endings.

But Lawrence had his sense of end too, aside from the apocalyptic ones in other works. Associated with completeness, it sometimes took the form of circularity and verticality: "A completed thought was the plumbing of a depth like a whirlpool, of emotional awareness, and at the depth of this whirlpool of emotion the resolve formed. But it was no stage in a journey. There was no logical chain to be dragged further" (*Apocalypse*, 81). A few pages later, he describes the mind of the "pagan thinker or poet" as working with images set in motion, then as this one spins on like a top, going on to another, suggesting Ezra Pound's image-juxtaposition poetic (p. 86). The pagan idea of time, moreover, is interpreted as "moving in cycles" (p. 87). The point here is two-fold. Lawrence uses a figure—verticality—itself symbolic of his own ideological cast and thrust (downwards into the depth of being). He also introduces his own kind of end, one involving imagery and motion in process of resolution. Lawrence, in effect, is advancing the esthetic sensibility against the apocalyptic sensibility. If, as some *Revelation* scholars maintain, there is literary art in *Revelation*, art also functions figuratively in *Apocalypse* as an alternative to the explosive final solutions of apocalyptic.

Lawrence regarded the Etruscans in some respects as early Symbolists because of all the intellectual correspondences found throughout their religion and art. In *Apocalypse* he insists that these pre-or non-Hellenic peoples (including the Etruscans) were artists, or at least possessed an esthetic mode of apprehension. In regarding feeling as deepening until a fullness representing a consummation of consciousness is achieved, Lawrence ironically satisfies T. S. Eliot's artistic desideratum that, like the Metaphysical poets, we should feel with our thoughts, and think with our feelings.

What Lawrence's speculation about the "artistic" nature of the "pagan" mind has to do with *Revelation* brings us to the iconoclasm in *Apocalypse*. The fundamental assumption of Lawrence's iconoclasm was that *Revelation* incorporated a kind of palimpsest in which the life-vision of a less morally rigid, nonteleological mind was "written over" by a morally provincial, end-obsessed, compulsively vindictive mentality. Lawrence's speculation that John, though espousing the "new" mentality, was still sufficiently imbued with the old consciousness to have conveyed something of it through various symbols, images, and ciphers (the four Apocalyptic Beasts, key mystical numbers like 3, 4, 7, 12, 666, the dragon, the Whore of Babylon, and the Woman Clothed with the Sun, who Lawrence takes to be a variant of the Great Mother), is to some extent confirmed by the claim of such *Revelation* scholars as Charles and Farrar that John did borrow. The main contention here is that John did transmit "pagan" as well as Old Testament elements in his message. (I beg the question regarding the authenticity of John's authorship, an elaborately contended issue among students of *Revelation*, and a matter both beyond my competence and the scope of this study.)

Lawrence's iconoclasm becomes, for some, extreme near the end of *Apocalypse* when, by intimating that the old religious sensibility was nonanthropomorphic, he eliminates deity. The divine force was not a deified human or being; it resembled instead Lawrence's poetic of momentaneity:

> Today, it is almost impossible for us to realize what the old Greeks meant by god, or *theos*. Everything was *theos*; but even so, not at the same moment. At the moment, whatever *struck* you was god. If it was a pool of water, the very watery pool might strike you: then that was god; or faint vapour at evening rising might catch the imagination: then that was *theos*; or thirst might overcome you at the sight of the water: then the thirst itself was god; or you drank, and the delicious and indescribable slaking of thirst was the god; or you felt the sudden chill of the water as you touched it: and then another god came into being, 'the cold;... 'moist,' 'the hot,' 'the dry' were things in themselves, realities, gods, *theoi*.
>
> [*Apocalypse*, 84-85]

"... all the religions [since Socrates] have been," Lawrence adds acidly, "religions of the dead body and the postponed reward..." (p. 85). Heaven is on earth and the "first life" to those for whom divinity can manifest itself anywhere, anytime. This religious sensibility is conditioned by a world, as Lawrence conceives it, in which human beings lived close to each other and to the surrounding universe:

Lawrence: "A New Heaven and an Old Earth"

> . . . the very ancient world was entirely religious and godless. While men still lived in close physical unison, like flocks of birds on the wing . . . an ancient tribal unison in which the individual was hardly separated out, then the tribe lived breast to breast, as it were, with the cosmos . . . the whole cosmos was alive and in contact with the flesh of man, there was no room for the intrusion of the god idea. It was not till the individual began to feel separated off, not till he fell into awareness of himself, and hence into apartness; not, mythologically, till he ate of the Tree of Knowledge instead of the Tree of Life, and knew himself *apart* and separate, that the conception of a God arose, to intervene between man and the cosmos. [*Apocalypse*, 159-60]

This Golden Age idea, exemplifying a trenchant intuition equal in excellence to cerebration, has been singled out for stricture by R. E. Pritchard who scorns it as "a return from independent living to primary being in a condition of womb-like security, what Freud called the 'oceanic state.'"[21] It is a part of modern wisdom to see through an idea; yet such penetration often leads to intellectual and cultural reductionism. Professor Pritchard sees here a womb-retreat. Struck by the salient Freudian contours of this passage, he overlooks an even more important feature: the inherent maturity of a mystical polity (as visualized by Lawrence) that did not experience an anxiety about existence sufficiently radical to create the need for a deified father-protector. If Lawrence's communal conception of *theos* merely amounts to an infantile regression, a sense of personified deity could be judged even more harshly.

Taking up John Burnet's *Early Greek Philosophers* again in order to compare the ideas of some pre-Socratic philosophers about the essential nature of the universe with Lawrence's, further supports the latter's iconoclastic claim that *Revelation* contains a kind of ancient thinking: "Anaximander taught . . . that there was an eternal, indestructible something out of which everything arises, and into which everything returns; a boundless stock from which the waste of existence is continually made good."²² Nondeifically called the Boundless, this "indestructible something" would later be regarded as God. An associate of Anaximander, Anaximenes, developed this concept of a nondeific divine substance by declaring that "the underlying substance was one and infinite . . . it was air" (p. 73). "The air," continues Burnet, "Anaximenes speaks of includes a good deal that we should not call by that name. In its normal condition . . . it is invisible, and it then corresponds to our 'air'; it is the breath we inhale and the wind that blows" (p. 74). What follows provides another example of an early, pre-Socratic philosophy resembling (and probably influencing) Lawrence's "dynamic consciousness," in which one lives intimately with the universe: "Just as our soul, being air, holds us together, so do breath and air encompass the whole world. The primary substance bears the same relation to the life of the world as to that of man. Now this was the Pythagorean view; it is also an early instance of the argument from the microcosm to the macrocosm . . . " (p. 75).

Lawrence asserts that the pre-Socratic philosophers like Anaxagoras had no conception of "the lengths to which mental activity could be carried" (*Apocalypse*, p. 76). Lawrence most probably depended on Burnet for the confidence with which he could make such generalizations and for much of his other information about these philosophers.²³ But he leaves Burnet behind when he goes on to say that

> . . . we have not the faintest conception of the vast range that was covered by the ancient sense-consciousness. We have lost almost entirely the great and intricately developed sensual awareness, or sense-awareness, and sense-knowledge, of the ancients. It was a great depth of knowledge arrived at direct, by instinct and intuition, as we say, not by reason. It was a knowledge based not on words but on images. The abstraction was not into generalisations or into qualities, but into symbols. And the connection was not logical but emotional. The word 'therefore' did not exist.
>
> [Pp. 76-77]

One also detects again the underlying Symbolist doctrine. Lawrence could almost be describing the structure of a poem by Mallarme.

Just as important, Lawrence's borrowing from Burnet proffers objective evidence for his own contentions about the religious meaning of *theos* and the cast of mind of pre-Classical peoples.[24] These early Greek philosophers regarded elemental substances (the Four Roots or four elements of Empedocles) as cosmological forces, creators, and sustainers of life (*Apocalypse*, p. 168). Whether Lawrence builds on these philosophers (or on Burnet) is less significant than what he builds on them—a vivid conception of the human mind, and of experience, existence, and the universe. Lawrence had a jeering yet at times refreshing disrespect for conventionally accepted interpretations by high-placed academics, and resists any "vested interest" readings that would deprive *Revelation* of its "heathen" properties. "John of Patmos is a Christian saint, so he *couldn't* have had any heathenism in mind. This is what orthodox criticism of *Revelation* amounts to. Whereas a matter of fact, we are amazed at the almost brutal paganism of 'our author,' John of Patmos. Whatever else he was, he was not afraid of a pagan symbol, nor even apparently, of a whole pagan cult. The old religions were cults of vitality, potency, and power: we must never forget it" (*Apocalypse*, pp. 58-59). As the idea of power is a complex and important constituent in both *Revelation* and *Apocalypse*, it is essential to discuss the form power takes in both works, for this theme is a touchstone of much that is disturbing and central in the Johannine and the Lawrencean revelation.

IV

Lawrence regards Christianity as consisting of two classes of people. The first includes strong individualists like Christ, aristocrats of the spirit who in their fullness of being can afford self-denial and altruism. The second and lower class, the spiritual plebeians, possess little or no individuality: "The mass of men live and move, think and feel collectively, and have practically no individual emotions, feelings or thoughts at all. They are fragments of the collective or social consciousness. It has always been so. And will always be so" (*Apocalypse*, p. 193). The aristocrats fulfill themselves by renunciation and serving the poor. "Well and good. But whom are the poor going to serve? It is a grand question. And John of Patmos answered it. The poor are going to serve themselves, and attend to their own self-glorification. And by the poor we don't mean the indigent *merely* [italics added]; we mean the merely collective souls. . . who have no aristocratic singleness and aloneness" (pp. 23-24). This passage is complexly ambivalent, as it contains valid charges against ideological self-serving elements in *Revelation*, as well as Lawrence's own abiding snobbery (which culminates in ideological axioms enunciated in the last chapter of *Apocalypse*). I will address myself to Lawrence's assault upon power in *Revelation*.

One can disagree with both Lawrence and Norman Cohn's evaluation of chiliasts. Cohn appears insufficiently sympathetic to the concrete human plight of these people, and Lawrence can be as socially vicious as a member of Proust's Verdurin set ("Down among the uneducated people," he says, as if peering down an Eastwood mine pit, "you will still find Revelation rampant " (p. 10). Two chapters later, Lawrence describes *Revelation* as having "had a greater effect on second-rate people throughout the Christian ages, than any other book in the Bible" (p. 20). Shortly after, he berates *Revelation* and John himself: "The Apocalypse of John is, as it stands, the work of a second-rate mind."

But some of Lawrence's insights into the power lust pervading *Revelation* possess the accuracy and originality of superior iconoclasm. He discerns this power drive in the

Christian doctrine of love: "Even Jesus was going to reign 'hereafter,' when his 'love' would be turned into confirmed power. This business of reigning in glory hereafter went to the root of Christianity, and is, of course, only an expression of frustrated desire to reign here and now" (p. 21). After briefly describing Jewish messianism as a longing for a world-conquering Messiah, Lawrence turns on the Christians: "The Christians took this up as the Second Advent of Christ, when Jesus was coming to give the gentile world its final whipping, and establish a rule of saints. John of Patmos extended this previously modest rule of saints (about forty years) to the grand round number of a thousand years, and so the Millenium took hold of the imagination of men" (p. 21). This passage culminates in a stark transvaluative indictment of the absolute greed for power in *Revelation*:

> And so there crept into the New Testament the grand Christian enemy, the power-spirit. At the very last moment, when the devil had been so beautifully shut out, in he slipped, dressed in apocalyptic disguise, and enthroned himself at the end of the book as Revelation.
> For Revelation . . . is the revelation of the undying will-to-power in man, and its sanctification, its final triumph. If you have to suffer martyrdom, and if all the universe has to be destroyed in the process, still, still, still, O Christian, you shall reign as a king and set your foot on the necks of the old bosses!
> This is the message of Revelation. [P. 22]

In electing Satan as the real cynosure of such celestial assemblages as "Salvation to our God which sitteth upon the throne and unto the Lamb. And all the angels stood round about the throne, and about the elders and the four beasts, and fell before the throne on their faces, and worshipped God. . . ." (Rev. 7: 10-11). Lawrence reveals the extremity and violence of his iconoclasm.

It would be appropriate here to cite passages in *Revelation* that test the veracity of Lawrence's case against the abuse of power in Christian apocalyptic. One significant pattern emerging is the juxtaposition of passages of abysmal suffering for the evildoers with descriptions of jubilant celebration among the virtuous. We get a foretaste of some of the Last Things to come at the opening of the sixth seal:

> . . .lo, there was a great earthquake; and the sun became black as sackcloth of hair; and the moon became as blood; and the stars of heaven fell unto the earth. . . . and every mountain and island were moved out of their places. And the kings of the earth, and the great men, and the rich men, and the chief captains, and the mighty men, and every bondsman, and every free man, hid themselves in the dens and in the rocks of mountains; And said to the mountains and rocks, Fall on us, and hide us from the face of him that sitteth on the throne, and from the wrath of the Lamb: For the great day of his wrath is come; and who shall be able to stand? [6: 12-17]

This cataclysmic wrath of the "Lamb" portends the mercilessness of the vengeance. Shortly before the seven last plagues are cast upon the wicked of the world after "Babylon" has been punished (for making "all nations drink of the wine of the wrath of her fornication"), we are told that any man who worships "the beast and his image," shall "be tormented with fire and brimstone in the presence of the holy angels, and in the presence of the lamb: and they have no rest day nor night, who worship the beast and his image" (14: 9-11). Anyone then who gave allegiance to the "beast" Domitian instead of to the Church would receive eternal torture. The "smoke" of their torment, with its modern connotations of Buchenwald and Dachau, is of course the (eternally) burning bodies of the evil, or, at least, the nonbelievers—all this with the Lamb and the angels looking on, presumably enjoying the incineration; as Dr. Martin Rist rather archly puts it in his "Introduction" to *Revelation in the Interpreter's Bible:* " . . .

the invoking of the vengeance and judgment of God against their persecutors by the martyrs might be considered to be unethical when judged by the highest Christian standards."[25]

Cosmic catastrophe recurs in one of the most destructive passages in *Revelation* with the tormented getting back at their tormentors (and the first-century "have-nots" through fantasy at the "haves")—the pouring out of six of the seven vials of the "wrath of God" upon the world:

> And I heard a great voice out of the temple saying to the seven angels, Go your ways, and pour out the vials of the wrath of God upon the earth.
>
> And the first went, and poured out his vial upon the earth; and there fell a noisome and grievous sore upon the men which had the mark of the beast. . . .
>
> And the second angel poured out his vial upon the sea; and it became as the blood of a dead man; and every living soul died in the sea. . . .
>
> For they have shed the blood of saints and prophets. . . . And the fourth angel poured out his vial upon the sun; and power was given unto him to scorch men with fire.
>
> And men were scorched with great heat, and blasphemed the name of God, which hath power over these plagues; and they repented not to give him glory. [16: 1-9]

Granted, the wicked ones "repented not to give him glory," but what an overkill for stubbornness.

Other passages of ferocious and lunatic revengefulness can be located in *Revelation*; I will mention only two. One concerns an angel who casts his "sharp sickle" into the earth. The "fruit" of this "cultivation"—cast into "the great winepress of the wrath of God"—is "blood [that] came out of the winepress, even unto the horse bridles, by the space of a thousand and six hundred furlongs" (14: 18-20). This destruction machine, which sounds more efficient than if not as mechanically intricate as Kafka's, has a yield of 352,000 yards of blood. That we are dealing with tormentors and executors of faithful (to Gibbon, obstinate) Christians might to an impartial observer seem to be outweighed by the titanic scope of this eschatological blood-lust. When Babylon is destroyed (in the subtle future-made-present, wish-fulfillment strategy of *Revelation*), the losers mourn, while the victors, heaven, the apostles and prophets, are urged to "Rejoice over her" (18: 19-20).

Even the dissenting reader of *Revelation* is threatened, drawn willy-nilly into the circle of unbridled retaliation at the end of *Revelation*: " . . . if any man shall add unto these things, God shall add unto him the plagues that are written in this book: And if any man shall take away from the words of the book of this prophecy, God shall take away his part out of the book of life, and out of the holy city . . ." (22: 18-19). Like too many ideologues, John tolerates no critics or sceptics.[26]

What does Lawrence think of this cosmic swathe of divine retribution? "It is very nice, if you are poor and *not* humble . . . to bring your grand enemies down to utter destruction and discomfiture, while you yourself rise up to grandeur." (*Apocalypse*, p. 12). "John the Divine," Lawrence continues, "had . . . a grandiose scheme for wiping out and annihilating everybody who wasn't of the elect . . ." (p. 13). This elect Lawrence identifies as both the lower-class early Christians and the Non-Conformist "chapel people" of Northern England. The apocalyptic triumph of the Lamb "is a doctrine you can hear any night from the Salvation Army or in any Bethel or Pentecost Chapel" (p. 13).

Lawrence's secular interpretation of the power struggle (or vacuum) in the first century A.D., probably influenced by Nietzsche, is closely tied to his elitist mystique: "In Jesus' day, the inwardly strong men everywhere had lost their desire to rule on earth. They wished to withdraw their strength from earthly rule and earthly power, and to apply it to another form of life. Then the weak began to rouse up and to feel *inordinately* conceited, they began to express their rampant hate of the 'obvious' strong ones, the men in worldly power" (*Apocalypse*, p.17)[27] Such attitudes about the "strong" and the "weak" surface a number of times in *Apocalypse*, and should be judged in the context of Lawrence's conservative and collectivist polity that culminates in the last chapter of his book. One might in passing isolate a crucial assumption made by Lawrence in his hierarchic social-moral structure. In insisting that "If the weak are not ruled, they will rule. . . . And the rule of the weak is *Down with* the strong!" he covertly identifies the terms "weak" and "poor" as readily interchangeable, an assumption no libertarian would grant (*Apocalypse*, pp. 17-18).

Lawrence time after time arraigns *Revelation* for its vindictive violence: "The second half of the Apocalypse is a flamboyant hate and simple lust . . . for the end of the world. The apocalyptist *must* see the universe . . . wiped out utterly, and merely a heavenly city and a hellish lake of brimstone left" (*Apocalypse*, p. 51). To Lawrence, it is all "bottom-dog" envy and retaliation. Yet he makes a telling point in his description of the Jesus Christ of *Revelation*: "Kosmokrator and Kosmodynamos.[28] Always the titles of power, and never the titles of love. Always Christ the omnipotent conqueror flashing his great sword and destroying, destroying vast masses of men, till blood mounts up the horses' bridles. Never Christ the Saviour; never" (*Apocalypse*, pp. 52-53).

A major passage of Lawrentian contempt and ire towards apocalyptic revenge suggests *Revelation* as the source of the doctrine of incessant punishment for the evil (that is, not only the religious oppressor, but also the happy or successful); it also indicates a noteworthy if slender vein of humanitarianism for which Lawrence seldom gets credited:

> This pleasant place [the "lake of fire burning with brimstone"] is the prototype of the Christian hell, specially

invented by the Apocalypse. The old Jewish hells of Sheol and Gehenna were fairly mild, uncomfortable abysmal places like Hades, and when a New Jerusalem was created from heaven, they disappeared. . . .
This was not good enough for the brimstone apocalyptist and John of Patmos. They must have a marvellous, terrific lake of sulphurous fire that could burn for ever and ever, so that the souls of the enemy could be kept writhing. When, after the last Judgment, earth and sky and all creation were swept away, and only glorious heaven remained, still, away down, there remained this burning lake of fire in which the souls were suffering. Brilliant glorious eternal heaven above: and brilliant sulphurous torture-lake away below. This is the vision of eternity of all Patmossers. They could not be happy in heaven unless they *knew* their enemies were unhappy in hell.

[*Apocalypse*, pp. 119-120]

A statement that once again polarizes Lawrence and Engels will round off this representation of Lawrence's attitude towards apocalyptic hatred and its motivations: "By the time of Jesus, all the lowest classes and mediocre people had realised that *never* would they get a chance to be kings, *never* would they go in chariots, never would they drink wine from gold vessels. Very well then—they would have their revenge by *destroying* it all" (*Apocalypse* , pp. 187-89).

These sentiments, according to Lawrence, culminate in a contradictory and deadly doubleness in Christian moral thought, represented by Jesus and John. "There is Christian love—and there is Christian envy. The former would save the world—the latter will never be satisfied till it has destroyed the world. They are two sides of the same medal" (*Apocalypse*, p. 189).

Though understandably attractive to large numbers of people born into and fettered by suffering, deprivation, and deliberate societal cruelty, the explosive, chiliastic violence of *Revelation* is regarded by Lawrence primarily as the vindictive expectations of permanently inadequate human beings—"*fragmentary* beings, *incapable* of whole individuality" (p. 190). So Lawrence dismisses them. It should be made clear that Lawrence does not *approve* of mass suffering. But one can demur at his solution or alternative, located with singular vividness in several passages. Man when alone is "a Christian, a Buddhist. . . . When he is with other men, instantly distinctions occur, and levels are formed. As soon as he is with other men Jesus is an aristocrat, a master. . . . So it is! Power is there, and always will be. . . . It is inevitable. Accept it, recognize the natural power in the man, as men did in the past, and give it homage, then there is great joy, and uplifting, and a potency passes from the powerful to the less powerful" (*Apocalypse*, pp. 24-25). (One might ask how many men or women possess the spiritual power of a Christ.)

Lawrence blurs the arbitrariness and social verticality of this leader-follower mystique, claiming at one point that aristocrats are composed of brave people (*Apocalypse*, p. 32). Suggesting *inner* nobility, this is at first disarming. In view further of Lawrence's profound ambivalence toward the lower *and* upper classes, it is difficult to determine what the credentials of men of power would be in his world (beyond resembling the Lawrentian). Such credentials would probably be so hard to transfer from Lawrence's "carbon" microcosm to the "coal-diamond-dust" macrocosm of the everyday world that we are not likely to be in danger of a Lawrentian elitist leadership.[29] This saving possibility is amplified by Baruch Hochman whose book *Another Ego* is generally critical of Lawrence's social ideology: "*Apocalypse* refers very clearly to a mystical rather than a political community."[30] Horace Gregory's insight is also pertinent: "In reading the last pages of *Apocalypse* we must remind ourselves that the only power Lawrence respected was the power of creation. All manipulation of that power towards other ends awakened his bitterest distrust."[31]

Although these words of Hochman and Gregory are reassuring, Kermode also has words worth heeding, which, directly concerned with Yeats, bear on Lawrence as well:

Yeats was enthusiastic for Italian fascism, and supported

an Irish fascist movement. The most terrible element in apocalyptic thinking is its certainty that there must be universal bloodshed; Yeats welcomed this with something of the passion that has attended the thinking of more dangerous because more practical men. 'Send war in our time, O lord.' Soon the towns lay beaten flat, and the great mass experiment in eugenics began. The dreams of apocalypse, if they usurp waking thought, may be the worst dreams.

At [sic] a poet, Yeats, at his best, was proof against enchantment by the dream. As a thinker outside poetry he was not; the only reason why this is unimportant is that he had no influence upon those who might have put his beliefs to an operational test.[32]

Lawrence in *Apocalypse* is not quite as vulnerable to the serious charges Kermode is making here against Yeats. Yet we know from such works as *The Plumed Serpent* and the essay "Reflections on the Death of a Porcupine" what Lawrence's polity can resemble, despite the trappings of art, or a mystical conception of a "benevolent" power, or some valid criticisms of democracy. Lawrence may have been suspicious of power manipulations, but his own ideal of the distribution of power in the real world can at best only be termed mystical; one could otherwise call it romanticized theocracy, or worse.[33]

V

A basic contention in this chapter is that *Apocalypse* is antiapocalyptic, a remarkable trait in view of the importance of apocalyptic in Lawrence's modes of thinking and creating as a literary artist. This antiapocalyptic strain is no less remarkable for its appearance in the iconoclastic *Apocalypse*, a work representing Lawrence's last opportunity to articulate and attract readers to his vision of life. To set forth the meaning of this gesture more vividly, I will briefly consider apocalyptic in Lawrence. A variety of apocalyptical materials appear throughout Lawrence's works, from "New Heaven and Earth," *The Rainbow*, and *Women in Love*, to *St. Mawr*, *The Plumed Serpent*, and *Lady Chatterley's Lover*. "Dies Irae" was one possible title for *Women in Love*, a novel full of personal and societal ends (and second beginnings, for the initiated). And *Lady Chatterley's Lover* begins with an ending and ends with a potentially "millenial" beginning. The apocalyptical has even been described as "the chief mould of Lawrence's imaginative activity," and Lawrence as a type of apocalyptic called Joachitic.[34]

Lawrence's own description of Joachitism in *Movements in European History* underlines his awareness of a popular, triadic apocalyptic that, as Cohn states, foresees the "Age of the Spirit" as the "culmination of human history":

> In 1254 a book was published called 'Introduction to the Everlasting Gospel,' supposed to contain the teaching of a famous seer or prophet, the abbot Joachim who had died at Naples in 1202. In this book it said that Judaism was the revelation of the Father; Christianity was the revelation of the Son: now men must prepare for the revelation of the Holy Ghost.
> Wild ideas spread everywhere. Men began to expect the reign of the Holy Ghost. They said that before Jesus was born the Father had reigned; after this, until their own day, the Son had reigned; now the Holy Ghost would reign. In the Everlasting Gospel, it was stated that when the Holy Ghost began to reign the papacy and the priesthood would cease to exist. There would be no more church to govern the souls of men. So the popes condemned the Everlasting Gospel as wicked, heretical, false doctrine. None the less it had a great power over the minds of men.[35]

The popularity and historicity of this heterodoxy, despite its support by the "masses," must have carried some weight with Lawrence.

In books like *Etruscan Places* and *Apocalypse*, one cannot discern any traces of Joachitism. In *Women in Love*, on the other hand, Lawrence's polarization of apocalyptic and scepticism assumes the form of "the historical tension between myth and history," or, on the corresponding plane of characters, the ideological wrangles between Birkin and Ursula.[36] Although Lawrence sometimes becomes irksomely tendentious when that tension relaxes or the pole of history (or novelistic realism) is omitted, his Joachitism can be effective in the context of literary interpretation. A good example is the apocalyptical peroration of the "*Moby Dick*" chapter in *Studies in Classic American Literature*, which, describing the "Last Day of White Civilisation in the fanatical pursuit of the White Whale," is Joachitic and yet compelling as visionary truth:

> Doom! Doom! Doom! Something seems to whisper it in the very dark trees of America. Doom! Doom of what? Doom of our white day. We are doomed, doomed. And the doom is in America. . . . Melville knew. He knew his race was doomed. His white soul doomed. His great white epoch, doomed. Himself, doomed. The idealist, doomed. The spirit, doomed. The reversion. 'Not so much bound to any haven ahead, as rushing from all havens astern'. The last ghastly hunt. The White Whale. What then is Moby Dick?—He is the deepest blood-being of the white race. He is our deepest blood-nature. . . . The last phallic being of the white man. Hunted into the death of upper consciousness and the ideal will. Our blood self subjected to our will.[37]

This passage displays how deeply Lawrence's mind could be imbued with apocalyptic, and what perceptiveness could be achieved by his strange blend of Joachitic eschatology, psychic ideology, and close reading of the text. The presence of apocalyptic elements in such works as *St. Mawr*, *The Plumed Serpent*, and *Lady Chatterley's Lover* accentuates by contrast the antiapocalyptic signature of Lawrence's last full-length doctrinal prose, as well as of *The Man Who Died*.

In his conceptualization about the Old World sensibility, Lawrence speculates about the original nature of the four Beasts of the Apocalypse and the cosmos from which they derive, a "cosmos that was not created, that had yet no god in it because it was in itself utterly divine and primal. Away behind all the creation myths lies the grand idea that the cosmos *always was*, that it could not have had any beginning, because it always was there and always would be there" (*Apocalypse*, p. 165).

When one eliminates beginnings, he potentially eliminates endings as well. As we cannot even conceive apocalyptically without an idea of an ending, Lawrence's idea is antiapocalyptic and also antianthropomorphic. To be sure, something can possibly be destroyed that has existed immemorially, but if one accepts the interpretation of *Revelation* as a great unified whole in which the ending is foreseen in the beginning and forms an insuperable apotheosis, then Lawrence knocks the bottom out by claiming that there was no beginning set off by a deity; the grand design is spoiled. And, as we have seen, he despises the ending ("How one loathes them [the saints and martyrs in *Revelation*], in their 'new white garments'" (p. 187)). Hilarious to some readers, it might strike others as impudent, nor is it as humane as could be desired ("it is not the revenge one minds so much . . . "—Why isn't it? (p. 187)). But the "perpetual self-glorification" galls Lawrence. One discovers here, as elsewhere, if he tries to read Lawrence without strong prepossessions, a sense of a proportion, degree, qualities of balance and sobriety his detractors insist he grossly lacked. Throughout *Apocalypse*, Lawrence registers evidence of a profound inadequacy in *Revelation* and, by extension, in the apocalyptical mentality—the absence of balance, the frenzied hatred, the craving for revenge, the schizophrenic promises to the faithful, the paranoic, demagogic lies about an apocalyptic utopia (where "there shall be no light" (*Revelation* 21: 25), for "The Lord God giveth them light; and they shall reign for ever and ever" (22:5).

But nothing reigns forever, including daylight and a "happy age." In creative opposition to Lawrence's own penchant to apocalyptic, one can find throughout his work an acute awareness of finitude, transience, change, limits, a natural rather than a supernatural sense of beginnings and ends. Measured by this sense of the natural, the vision of apocalyptic *is* a fantasy, and a dangerous one, despite Engel's humane perspective.

Yet how much should one condemn apocalyptical visions or hallucinations, particularly if they can clearly be shown, as Engels adduces, to result from societal oppression? Organized society, as a socioeconomic configuration of concentrated power, is culpable for the psychotic preternaturalism inherent in apocalyptical thought and action. If apocalyptic sublimates almost unendurable social and personal suffering, the vision or fantasy produced by it possesses a value superior to the spurious anodynes of modern mass culture. The choice, however, is not between television-beer-football-cars on the one hand, and revolution on the other. It is between revolution and regeneration. And though these two potentially apocalyptic modes need not figure antithetically, Lawrence, in the generally individualist nature of his search as an artist for consummation, opts for regeneration.[38]

Both Lawrence's and Cohn's strictures of apocalypse have merit. Whatever extenuating circumstances might (and should) make one sympathetic toward people driven by desperation to apocalypse, and hostile toward the "Romans" who create the secular conditions inspiring such desperation, all socially-activated apocalyptical thought can terminate in excess and even in holocaust, imposing a "dream" humanly worse than the living nightmare it was intended to replace.

VI

"In the Apocalypse," claims Norman O. Brown, "the walls do fall; the wall separating inside and outside; public and private; body physical and metaphysical. The identification of sex and politics . . ."[39] At its best, *Revelation* posits a reversi-

Lawrence: "A New Heaven and an Old Earth" 161

ble transformation in sensibility; the revelation is a revolution, and the revolution is a revelation. John R. May puts one side of it succinctly yet suggestively: "Apocalyptic literature . . . uses the mythic framework of the regeneration of the world as a macrocosmic idiom for another important Christian concern, *metanoia* [regeneration] of the individuial."[40] Lawrence would not have seen *Revelation* in this light. His case for the pathological character of the last book of the New Testament is cogent. Yet it cannot be doubted that for some people *Revelation* did inspire a change of heart, a coiling of energy through a fideistic self-renunciation, which, sprung, unleashed a new dimension of self or being. The fact that *Revelation* did this at the point of an ideological sword cannot completely detract from its facet of individual and communal regeneration. The critical question is how personal regeneration and social revolution are relatable. Are they interchangeable? Or does a coarsening occur—Joseph Conrad's "degradation of the idea"—in the movement from the personal to the social experience? The concept of communality can so be defined as to assure the retention of individual integrity in a social context. But this merely defines an ideal. And although Lawrence went through periods of seeking such communality as Rananim or his Etruscan golden age or a durable fellowship with a John Middleton Murry, he always returned to his "cult" of the self, though sometimes with a female partner. In *Apocalypse* he does not confront the issue of the potential interchangeability of personal transformation and social revolution. Using John of Patmos, the "moralistic Jews," and the Midlands "Chapel folk" as butts, he derides rather than analyzes the problem. He sees keenly through the hysterical inhumanity of apocalyptic and is unpleasantly outspoken about the possible unchangeability of most people (let alone the poor). For all his creativity with ideas and experiences of flux, movement, and change, Lawrence's thought becomes impacted and unfertile when dealing with the possibility of self-development for certain strata of humanity.

Lawrence's most compelling objection to apocalyptic regeneration—one far superior to his elitist, hierarchical criteria for rejecting *Revelation*—is broadly religious. Eugene Goodheart phrases it concisely: "... Christianity involves the transcendence of the idea of resurrection. Man is to rise to a place in the eternal scheme of things never to rise again. To Lawrence the rhythm of death and rebirth is an eternal rhythm which can never be transcended so long as there is life. Lawrence consequently loathed the idea of immortality."[41] I would disgree with Goodheart's formulation in one respect. Lawrence affirmed and frequently dramatized the idea of psychic or symbolic immortality in terms of a transcendence of the ego, the "I-obsessed" self which he identified with cerebral consciousness. Only lapse out, his partial alter ego Rupert Birkin tells the ego-incarcerated Hermione. Further, Lawrence's concept of the eternality of "the rhythm of life and death" clearly connotes a kind of immortality. But another sort of immortality that Lawrence calls "the magnificent here and now of life in the flesh," emerges climactically in *Apocalypse* itself:

> By the very frenzy with which the Apocalypse destroys the sun and the stars, the world, and all kings and all rulers, all scarlet and purple and cinnamon, all harlots, finally all men together who are not 'sealed,' we can see how deeply the apocalyptists are yearning for the sun and the stars and the earth and the waters of the earth, for nobility and lordship and might, and scarlet and gold splendour, for passionate love, and a proper unison with men, apart from this sealing business. What man most passionately wants is his living wholeness and his living unison, not his own isolate salvation of his 'soul.' . . . the magnificent here and now of life in the flesh is ours, and ours alone, and ours only for a time. We ought to dance with rapture that we should be alive and in the flesh, and part of the living, incarnte cosmos. . . .
> So that my individualism is really an illusion. I am a part of the great whole, and I can never escape. [Pp. 199-200]

This famous passage suggests immortality not as rebirth,

but as so deep and body-mystically a faith in one's life as organic, communal relatedness to the surrounding world as to approach the estate of a "new life." But this "lapsing out" must also be viewed as integral to Lawrence's attack on libertarian, democratic individualism ("my individualism," he says, including even his "Salvator Mundi" self in the cancellation).

Such a peculiar combination of an exciting immortalization of the living moment with an accentuated elitism presents the final obstacle in judging *Apocalypse* as a cultural document. Lawrence's individualism *was* an illusion only as *he* saw it embodying human disconnection. As a symbolic gesture expressed in numerous significant literary works of the holy need to cut away from a destructive modern world, his individualist metaphysic served a viable purpose. It embodied the heterocosm of a slender yet invaluable communality, a "mystic marriage" in which the tension of free wills and developing being ineluctably precluded risk of autocracy of any sort. This "second world," akin to the "art world" of the Symbolist esthetic, could be willed into existence only by first being conceived by a creative *mind*, by *his* creative mind, whether "part of the great whole" or not. Lawrence, all the snobbery and mystagogy aside, is striving to preserve something precious in *Apocalypse*. "St. John said," he states in *The Symbolic Meaning*, " 'There shall be no more sea.'"[42] A recent student of *Revelation* has observed that John might have regarded the sea as symbolic of evil, danger, and distress.[43] But Lawrence's response to John the Divine's promise or threat of colossal evaporation is profoundly, humanly evaluative, a Lawrentian judgment of apocalyptical dispensations toward the "old" earth: "St. John said, 'there shall be no more sea.' That was esoteric. Exoterically, Dana and Melville say the same. The Sea, the great Waters, is the material home of the deep sacral-sexual consciousness. To the very depths of his home Melville pursues the native consciousness in himself, and destroys it there. When he has really destroyed this sacral-sexual consciousness, destroyed or over-thrown it, then John's prophecy will be fulfilled. There will be no more sea."

To Lawrence, John the Divine and the apocalyptist ethos threaten the unconscious itself, the "sea" of impulse, instinct, intuition, the vast reserve of energy and will to new or creative life. For all his intemperateness and, at times, rank inhumanity, Lawrence experienced life at its essence, and so crystallized it imaginatively as to shatter all forms of inhuman stratification that would prevent human beings from making the revelation a revolution against synthetics ends and disoriented beginnings. That much that lies in between would thus benefit remains a noble ideal, and one for which Lawrence deserves more praise than he has received.

Notes

Note: All references in this essay to the text of D. H. Lawrence's *Apocalypse* are from the 1966 Viking Compass Book edition.

1. See L. D. Clark ("The Apocalypse of Lorenzo," The *D. H. Lawrence Review* vol 3, p. 2 (Summer, 1970): p. 141-60, for a lucid treatment of symbolic and esoteric qualities in *Apocalypse*, of its relation to the apocalyptic tradition, and of the problem in that tradition of the schism between literal and symbolic meanings. Helen Corke's short book, *D. H. Lawrence and Apocalypse* (London: Heinemann, 1933), is more of a personal rather than scholarly commentary on both *Apocalypse* and Lawrence himself.

2. Lawrence for example describes a death-rebirth ceremony in Chapter 2 and calls it a "ritual of the Mysteries of Isis," which he correlates with the opening of the seventh seal (*Apocalypse*, p. 108).

3. Austin Farrar, *A Rebirth of Images: The Making of St. John's Apocalypse* (Boston: Beacon Press, 1963), p. 6.

4. R. H. Charles, *A Critical and Exegetical Commentary on the Revelation of St. John* (Edinburgh: T. H. Clark, 1920), p. clxxxvi.

5. D. H. Lawrence, *Phoenix: The Posthumous Papers of D. H. Lawrence*, ed. by Edward McDonald, 1936 (New York: Viking Press, 1972), p. 294.

6. Hubert J. Richards, *What the Spirit Says to the Churches: A Key to the Apocalypse of John* (New York: P. J. Kennedy and Sons, 1967), p. 136.

7. Frank Kermode, *The Sense of an Ending: Studies in the Theory of Fiction* (London: Oxford University Press, 1968), p. 5.

8. John R. May, *Toward a New Earth: Apocalypse in the American Novel* (Notre Dame, Ind.: University of Notre Dame Press, 1973), pp. 17-18.

9. Kermode, *The Sense of an Ending*, p. 6.

10. Madeleine S. Miller and J. Lane Miller, *Harper's Biblical Dictionary* (New York: Harper & Row, 1952), pp. 614-15.

11. Norman Cohn, *The Pursuit of the Millenium* (Fairlawn, New Jersey: Essential Books Inc., 1957), p. 4.
12. Lewis Feuer, ed., *Basic Writings on Politics and Philosophy: Karl Marx and Friedrich Engels* (Garden City, New York: Doubleday, 1959), pp. 183-84.
13. Norman Cohn, *The Pursuit of the Millenium*, p. 309.
14. Frederick Carter, *D. H. Lawrence and the Body Mystical* (London: Archer, 1932, p. 54. See also Harry T. Moore, *The Priest of Love: A Life of D. H. Lawrence* (New York: Farrar, Straus, and Cudahy, 1974), pp. 483, 493-94.
15. Eugene Goodheart, *The Utopian Vision of D. H. Lawrence* (Chicago: University of Chicago Press, 1963), p. 96.
16. Cf. Northrop Frye's hylozoism, "By an apocalypse I mean primarily the imaginative conception of the whole of nature as the content of an infinite and eternal living body, which, if not human, is closer to being human than to being inanimate." (*Anatomy of Criticism*, Princeton, N.J.: Princeton University Press, 1957, p. 119).
17. See James C. Cowan *D. H. Lawrence's American Journey* (Cleveland, Ohio: Case Western Reserve University Press, 1970), (chapter 2) for a lucid and concise discussion of Lawrence's system of the "plexuses" in *Fantasia of the Unconscious*.
18. D. H. Lawrence, *The Symbolic Meaning: The Uncollected Versions of Studies in Classic American Literature* (New York: Viking Press, 1964), pp. 68-70.
19. Goodheart, *The Utopian Vision of D. H. Lawrence*, p. 48. The conception of cult to culture as a degenerative process is discussed in an absorbing article by Jacob Taubes ("From Cult to Culture," *Partisan Review* vol 21, pt.4 (July-August, 1954): pp. 386-400). Dr. Taubes locates a radical conservative polyhistor and philosopher of culture in Thomas Mann's *Dr. Faustus* named Chaim Breisacher whose life counterpart, a man named Oskar Goldberg, interprets the "whole history of civilization as nothing but a process of decline from cult to culture" (p. 388). Breisacher-Goldberg's cultism, which posits a mystical, galvanizing relation between a nation's gods and the nation (or tribe) but which also asserts that man must first abolish the whole history of culture in order to recover social potency (p. 399), almost makes Lawrence's regressive tendencies seem moderate. Lawrence has indicated more than once that man cannot retreat into simpler modes of consciousness or stages of culture (although he has also intimated the opposite more than once).
20. Frank Kermode, "Lawrence and the Apocalyptic Types," in *D. H. Lawrence: The Rainbow and Women in Love*, ed. Colin Clarke (Nashville, London: Aurora Publishers, 1970), p. 209.
21. R. E. Pritchard, *D. H. Lawrence: Body of Darkness* (Pittsburgh, Penn.: University of Pittsburgh Press, 1971), p. 199.
22. John Burnet, *Early Greek Philosophers* (London: A. and C. Black, 1930), p. 53.
23. William York Tindall, *D. H. Lawrence and Susan his Cow* (New York: University of Columbia Press, 1939), p. 122. See also pp. 156-57, where Tindall argues that *Apocalypse* is a theosophical tract, heavily dependent on James Pryse and Madame Blavatsky ("Though it owes much to John Burnet's *Early Greek Philosophy*, Lawrence's *Apocalypse* is essentially a close adaptation of Pryse and Blavatsky." L. D. Clark restores to Lawrence's borrowings the dignity and seriousness that his detractors were ready enough to bestow upon those of Joyce, Eliot, and Yeats: "In his quest for closer correspondences than those afforded by the Christian tradition, he brought to his last book knowledge from a life-long study of paganism and oc-

cultism." ("The *Apocalypse* of Lorenzo"--p.149)

24. So does a more recent scholar of ancient Greek religion, W. K. C. Guthrie, *The Greeks and Their Gods*, (Boston: Beacon Press, 1955)), who, describing the "life-in-matter" Ionian philosophers, says that the idea of *theos* comes from their sense that the world is eternal, a condition linked with its hylozoistic, animate condition—"It must have been in this sense," Guthrie continues, "that Thales said that everything was full of gods . . . " (p. 135).

25. George A. Buttrick, *The Interpreter's Bible* vol. 12 (New York: Abingdon Press, 1957), p. 349.

26. Mr. William Klassen (in "Vengeance in the *Apocalypse* of John," *The Catholic Biblical Quarterly* 28 (1966): 300-11), offers various arguments in a clarificatory defense of Johannine revengefulness, such as that God's "battle is almost always portrayed as a defensive war" (p. 305), that "the saints are at no place depicted as enjoying forever the torture of their enemies" (p. 309), that "we must also get accustomed to seeing the concept of the wrath of God as central to the Christian faith" (p. 310). He also claims that "The stress is not on the delight in her [Babylon's] suffering but joy in the outcome of God's cause,"—p. 304). It remains a matter of opinion, nonetheless, on which side that stress falls, nor do any of the three preceding arguments in any way diminish the authorial or narrator vindictiveness in *Apocalypse*.

27. For recent articles comparing Nietzsche and Lawrence, see John B. Humma, "D. H. Lawrence as Fredrich Nietzsche," *Philological Quarterly* 53 (January 1974): 110-20, and Eleanor A. Green, "Blueprints for Utopia: The Political Ideas of Nietzsche and Lawrence," *Renaissance and Modern Studies* 18 (1974): 141-61. Humma quotes Nietzsche in *Twilight of the Gods* as insisting that "Socrates was a misunderstanding; the whole improvement morality, including the Christian, was a misunderstanding. . . . Lawrence might have written the same thing—and nearly did [in *Apocalypse*]. . . . In contrast to his contempt for the age of Socrates, he praises the old Greeks for their 'logic of action rather than reason'" (p. 115). The author of *Etruscan Places* would not have taken kindly, however, to Nietzsche's opinion in *The Genealogy of Morals* that "The Romans were the strongest and most noble people who ever lived" (p. 186, Anchor ed.).

28. Sandra Gilbert rightly speaks (in *Acts of Attention*, p. 272) of Lawrence's fondness in *Last Poems* for Kosmocrator and Kosmodynamos. Yet structurally significant in *Apocalypse* is his ideological polarization of the two deity concepts, and his hylozoistic exaltation of Kosmodynamos precisely for its primordial character as a nonhumanized force.

29. See Lawrence's famous letter to Edward Garnett for his exposition of the "coal-diamond-carbon" metaphor (*Collected Letters of D. H. Lawrence*, ed. by Harry T. Moore, New York: Viking Press, 1962 pp. 281-82).

30. Baruch Hochman, *Another Ego: The Changing View of Self and Society in the Works of D. H. Lawrence* (Columbia, S. C.: University of South Carolina Press, 1933), p. 222.

31. Horace Gregory, *Pilgrim of the Apocalypse* (New York: The Viking Press, 1933), p. 102.

32. Kermode, *The Sense of an Ending*, pp. 108-09.

33. Those ready to call it worse have never been lacking, of course, but few have done so in English from the standpoint of *approving* of Lawrence's "fascism." One

member of this set is an American professor of history named Stebleton H. Nulle who (in "D. H. Lawrence and the Fascist Movement," *The New Mexico Quarterly*, (February, 1940), pp. 3-15), regarding the leaders of Fascism doing for Lawrence's ideas what Paul did for Jesus (p. 5), makes other equally stunning pairings: "Just as Robespierre was Rousseau's finest pupil, one might say that Adolph Hitler is bringing into Western consciousness something of the insight and idealism of D. H. Lawrence" (p. 12). Eric Bentley, who is hostile to Lawrence's political ideas, nevertheless regards Lawrence (as I do) as divided between humanist and authoritarian values: "Consistency is not a Lawrentian virtue, and one finds in his anarchism, in his unwillingness to kill a fellow man, in his emphasis on tenderness, a rejection of fascist theory and fascist practise. Lawrence esteemed the individual above everything else, and he hoped that workmen, not simply a few individuals, would become true individuals . . ." (*A Century of Hero Worship*, p. 251). A refreshing antielitism during this period emerges in a poem from *Pansies* that begins: "When wilt thou teach the people, / God of justice, to save themselves--? / They have been saved so often and sold" (*The Complete Poems of D. H. Lawrence*, p. 442).

34. Kermode, "Lawrence and the Apocalyptic Types," p. 209.
35. Norman Cohn, *The Pursuit of the Millenium*, p. 100. D. H. Lawrence, *Movements in European History* (London: Oxford University Press, 1925), pp. 193-94.
36. Kermode, *Lawrence and the Apocalyptic Type*, p. 217. I am indebted to Kingsley Widmer for pointing out to me that Joachitism appears in Lawrence's work as early as *Twilight in Italy* (specifically in the chapters "The Lemon Gardens," "The Theatre," and, by implication, the concluding two pages of "The Spinner and the Monks").
37. D. H. Lawrence, *Studies in Classic American Literature*, (Garden City, New York: Doubleday, 1973), p. 173. Lawrence's Joachitism also appears in the Poe chapter in the same book: "The next era is the era of the Holy Ghost" (p. 89).
38. Denis Donoghue, like other commentators, fails to distinguish between revolution and regeneration in Lawrence, but he is clear and sympathetic in interpreting Lawrence's grasp of and preference for the Old to the New World mind: Lawrence "was not proposing to go back to astrology and augury, but to effect a revolution, a radical change of heart, for which astrology and augury were the merest approximations. He does not write of the modern world as if it had never happened, but as if it had now to be transfigured. Such transfiguration would be impossible in a scientific world governed by mechansim and the divided consciousness." (*Thievs of Prometheus*, New York: Oxford University Press, 121-22)
39. Norman O. Brown, *Love's Body* (New York: Random House, 1968), p. 126.
40. John R. May, *Toward a New Earth*, p. 23.
41. Eugene Goodheart, *The Utopian Vision of D. H. Lawrence*, p. 91.
42. Ibid.: p. 213.
43. J. Massingberde Ford, *Revelation: Introduction, Translation, and Commentary* (Garden City, New York: Doubleday, 1975), p. 36. See also V. Burch, *Anthropology and the Apocalypse* (London: Macmillan, 1939), who sees the abolition of the sea in *Revelation* as a Folk-cosmology mode by which Leviathan, or death, is destroyed in his own medium, which "has vanished with the third embodiment of Death" (pp. 159-60).

Conclusion

'Of course this death has been troubling me.'
'Aziz was so fond of her too.'
'But it has made me remember that we must all die; all these personal relations we try to live by are temporary. I used to feel death selected people. . . . Now "death spares no one" begins to be real.'
'Don't let it become too real, or you'll die yourself. That is the objection to meditating upon death. We are subdued to what we work in.'[1]

Cyril Fielding's warning in this conversation late in Forster's novel is not one that Lawrence violated. Lawrence in the last years was not subdued to death, in part because of the varieties of death that he "worked in." On the contrary, his heightened sense of personal, biological death must have generated some of the rebirth motifs in his last writings. A host of richly ambiguous symbolic renewals emerge through Lawrence's deft intermingling of figurative with literal death. As Chaman Nahal has observed, "For Lawrence the artist, one need not have to physically die to have the joy of the unknown. The unknown is ever there in life itself; every new moment, in its newness, is nothing but a representation of it. One needs only the capacity to die to the past moments to convey the richness of the new."[2]

Lawrence's sense of the reality of death has been alluded to earlier; this awareness lends fortitude to *Last Poems*. But rebirth itself is not an estate easily arrived at in Lawrence's works. A fine instance of this occurs in *Lady Chatterley's*

Conclusion

Lover. Mellors, like Connie only half-alive in the first section of the story, appraises the cost of new life in their beginning love affair: "'I thought I'd done with it all. Now I've begun again.' 'Begun what?' 'Life.' 'Life,' she re-echoed with a queer thrill. 'It's life,' he said. 'There's no keeping clear. And if you do keep clear you might almost as well die. So if I've got to be broken open again, I have.'"[3]

The pivotal words here are "broken open," which convey the acute ambivalence Mellors-Lawrence felt towards rebirth. No so dissimilar to Eliot's "April is the cruellest month," this passage reveals the committment of engaging another human being as a burden not lightly assumed. We behold an ailing author's reluctance to go on living, but also a dramatization of human reluctance to aspire to larger existence.

Nevertheless, a demon in Lawrence seems during these final years to have throbbed receptively to the sense of immortality that, according to Ernst Cassirer, possessed primitive man: "The conception that man is mortal . . . seems to be entirely alien to mystical and primitive religious thought."[4] This claim, combined with Cassirer's assertion that "Primitive religion is perhaps the strongest and most energetic affirmation of life that we find in human culture," gives one measure, social conservatism notwithstanding, of the force for life-renewal within Lawrence's mystical and mythical concerns.[5] The full value of Lawrence's primitivism has yet to be realized; the fact that it is integral to Lawrence's death-and-rebirth ideas at most suggests rather than measures its depths.[6]

Nearly dying in 1925 gave Lawrence a passport to death. He could almost go there, and return. This provided him with a two-world vision, rather than Rilke's "keeping life open to death."[7] Lawrence acquired thereby a unique and invigorating grasp on life. His death-and-rebirth preoccupations, far from being a facile evasion of death, become one with the mysticism of, as Dean Inge puts it, "the immanence of the temporal in the eternal, and of the eternal in the temporal."

It has been a contention in this study that the work of Lawrence's last four years is unified by his versatile use of death-and-rebirth materials. As we have seen, this activity assumes such forms as a girl's ritual passage toward adulthood, an exaltation of a Golden Age society, verse meditations on biological and figurative death and their transcendence. And it concludes Lawrence's career as an elitist attack on Biblical apocalyptic and a celebration of a Lawrentian ancient psyche and of finite existence. The fluid interaction of literal and symbolic death further relates these late works. In none of them is the conception of death single in meaning. This is equally true of the treatment of rebirth. The result is a wisdom literature of modes of mortality and immortality. Perhaps the ultimate gain results from neither mode dominating.

Lawrence's instinctualism or primitivism, in some ways hostile to intellect, cultivates a saving sense of our own mortality. By recognizing one's affinity with not only birds, beasts, and flowers, but even more elemental phenomena, salt, stone, water, air, ultimately the cosmos, man reenters his "place" in a vivid structure of animate and inanimate forces. Such a recognition, Lawrence felt, is profoundly enhancing. "We can never," he claimed, in a late review of Frederick Carter's *Dragon of the Apocalypse*, "recover an old vision, once it has been supplanted. But what we can do is to discover a new vision in harmony with the memories of old . . . far-off experience [sic] that lie within us. So long as we are not deadened or drossy, memories of Chaldean experience still live within us, at great depths and can vivify our impulses in a new direction, once we awaken them."[8] The thrust of Lawrence's best work, including some of the last writings, makes this "last will" an affirming and abiding one for any age beset by the specter of a personal and societal end devoid of another chance for creative existence.

Notes

1. E. M. Forster, *A Passage to India* (London: Edward Arnold & Co., 1949), p. 274.
2. Chaman Nahal, *D. H. Lawrence: An Eastern View*, (Cranbury, N.J.: A. S. Barnes, 1970) p. 256.
3. Ibid., p. 125 (Bantam edition).
4. Ernst Cassirer, *An Essay on Man* (Garden City, New York: Doubleday, 1953), p. 111.
5. Ibid., p. 112.
6. Timothy Longville, in "The Longest Journey: D. H. Lawrence's *Phoenix*," *Critical Quarterly* IV (Spring 1962), views Lawrence's primitivism as unreal and regressive: "Lawrence's vision of the world as it ought to be is of a recreated prelapsarian Eden" (p. 82). What truth resides in this stricture of Lawrence is vitiated by Longville's contention that Lawrence's mythic vision is not distinguishable from oblivion ("The confusion between Eden and oblivion constantly recurs in Lawrence's work . . ."--p. 83). In view of the sinewy interconnections one can discover throughout Lawrence's writings between oblivion, "lapsing out," apocalyptic, and a "recreated prelapsarian Eden," Longville begs the question by not amplifying the terms of his discussion of Lawrence's myth-making. For a cogent argument against interpreting Lawrence as an Edenic writer, one can consult James R. Baker, "D. H. Lawrence as Prophetic Poet," *Journal of Modern Literature* vol. 3, no. 5 (July 1974): 1234-35 ("He [Lawrence] did not look for a regressive apotheosis, but for recovery, a recovery of the full potentials of our being, and from that, he believed, the rest would follow"—p. 1238). Kingsley Widmer, in a discussion of Lawrence's primitivism, makes a useful distinction between the "primitivist" (or the primitive) and the "primitivistic" (*The Art of Perversity: D. H. Lawrence's Shorter Fiction* (Seattle, Wash.; University of Washington Press, 1962), pp. 29-31)
7. See *Sonnets to Orpheus*, ed. by M. D. Herter Norton (New York: Norton, 1962), pp. 130-32.
8. D. H. Lawrence, *Phoenix: The Posthumous Papers*, ed. by Edward McDonald. (New York: Viking Press, 1972), p. 301.

Selected Bibliography

Alvarez, A. "The Single State of Man." In *A. D. H. Lawrence Miscellany*. Edited by Harry T. Moore. Carbondale, Ill.: Southern Illinois University Press, 1959.

Bair, Hebe. "Lawrence as Poet." *The D. H. Lawrence Review* Volume 6, Number 3, (1973).

Banti, Luisa. *Etruscan Cities and their Culture*. Berkeley Calif.: University of California Press, 1973.

Bentley, Eric. *A Century of Hero Worship*. Philadelphia, Pa.: Lippincott, 1941.

Bloch, Raymond. *The Etruscans*. New York, N.Y.: Praeger, 1958.

―――.*Ancient Civilization of the Etruscans*. New York: Cowles Book Company, 1969.

Brewster, Earl, and Brewster, Achsah. *D. H. Lawrence, Reminescences and Correspondences*. London: Secker, 1934.

Brown, Norman O. *Life Against Death: A Psychoanalytic Interpretation of History*. New York: Random House, 1959.

―――.*Love's Body*. New York: Random House, 1966.

Burch, V. *Anthropology and the Apocalypse*. London: Macmillan, 1939.

Burnet, John. *Early Greek Philosophy*. London: H. & T. Black, 1930.

Burwell, Rose Marie. 1970. "A Catalog of D. H. Lawrence's Readings from Early Childhood." *The D. H. Lawrence Review*, Volume 3:3 (1970).

Buttrick, George A., *The Interpreter's Bible*, Vol. 13, New York: Abingdon Press, 1959.

Carter, Frederick. 1932. *D. H. Lawrence and the Body Mystical*. London: Archer.

Cavitch, David. *D. H. Lawrence and the New World*. New York: Oxford University Press, 1969.

Selected Bibliography

Cervantes, Miguel. *Don Quixote*. New York: New American Library, 1964.

Charles, R. H. *A Critical and Exegetical Commentary on the Revelation of St. John*. Edinburgh: T. H. Clarke, 1920.

Cipolla, Elizabeth. "The Last Poems of D. H. Lawrence, *The D. H. Lawrence Review*, Vol. 2, No. 2 (1969).

Clark, L. D. *Dark Night of the Body: D. H. Lawrence's The Plumed Serpent*. Austin, Tx: University of Texas Press, 1964.

―――."The Apocalypse of Lorenzo," *The D. H. Lawrence Review*. Vol. 3, No. 3 (1970).

Cles-Reden, Sibylle Von. *The Buried People: A Study of the Etruscan World*. London: Hart-Davis, 1955.

Cohn, Norman *The Pursuit of the Millenium*. Fairlawn,N.J.: Essential Books, Inc. 1957.

Corke, Helen. *D. H. Lawrence and Apocalypse*. London: Heinemann, 1933.

Cowan, James E. *D. H. Lawrence and the American Journey*. Cleveland, Ohio: Case Western Reserve Press, 1964.

Dennis, George. *The Cities and Cemeteries of Etruria*. London: John Murray, 1883.

Donoghue, Denis. *Thieves of Prometheus*. New York: Oxford University Press, 1974.

Elliott, Robert C. *The Shape of Utopia: Studies in a Literary Genre*. Chicago, Ill.: University of Illinois Press, 1970.

Farrar, Austin. *A Rebirth of Images: The Making of St. John's Apocalypse*. Boston: Beacon Press, 1963.

Feuer, Lewis. *Basic Writings on Politics and Philosophy: Karl Marx and Friedrich Engels*. Garden City, N.Y.: Doubleday, 1959.

Ford, George H. *Double Measure: A Study of the Novels and Stories of H. H. Lawrence*. New York: Holt, Rinehart, and Winston, 1965.

Ford, J. Massingberde. *Revelation: Introduction, Translation, and Commentary*. Garden City, N.Y.: Doubleday, 1975.

Frankfurt, Henri, et al. *Before Philosophy: The Intellectual Adventure of Ancient Man*. Harmondsworth, England: Penguin, 1949.

Freeman, Mary. "D. H. Lawrence in Valhalla." *The New Mexico Quarterly*. (1940): 211-24.

―――.*D. H. Lawrence: A Basic Study of his Ideas*. Gainesville,

Fla.: University of Florida Press, 1955.

Frye, Northrop. *Anatomy of Criticism*. Princeton, N.J.: Princeton University Press, 1957.

Gilbert, Sandra *Acts of Attention*. Ithaca, New York, and London: Cornell University Press, 1972.

Goodheart, Eugene. *The Utopian Vision of D. H. Lawrence*. Chicago: University of Chicago Press, 1963.

Green, Eleanor A. "Blueprints for Utopia: The Political Ideas of Nietzsche and Lawrence," *Renaissance and Modern Studies* vol. 18 (1974).

Gregory, Horace. *Pilgrim of the Apocalypse*. New York, N.Y.: Viking Press, 1933.

Guthrie, W. K. C. *The Greeks and Their Gods*. Boston, Mass.: Beacon Press, 1950.

Hampton, Christopher. *The Etruscan Survival*. Garden City, N. Y.: Doubleday, 1970.

Harrison, John R. *The Reactionaries*. New York, N.Y.: Schocken Books, 1967.

Hassall, Christopher. "D. H. Lawrence and the Etruscans," *Essays of Divers Hands* vol. 31 (1962) 61-78.

Hencken, Hugh. *Tarquinia and Etruscan Origins*. New York, Praeger, 1968.

Heurgon, Jacques. *Daily Life of the Etruscans*. London: Weidenfeld & Nicolson, 1964.

Hochman, Baruch. *Another Ego: The Changing View of Self and Society in the Work of D. H. Lawrence*. Columbia, S.C.: University of South Carolina Press, 1970.

Hoffman, Frederich J. *The Mortal No: Death and the Modern Imagination*. Princeton, N.J.: Princeton University Press, 1964.

Hough, Graham. *The Dark Sun: A Study of D. H. Lawrence*. London: Duckworth, 1956.

Humma, John B. "D. H. Lawrence as Fredrich Nietzsche," *Philological Quarterly* vol. 53 (1974).

Hus, Alain. *The Etruscans*. New York: Grove Press, 1961.

Huxley, Aldous. *The Letters of D. H. Lawrence*. New York: Viking Press, 1932.

Inniss, Kenneth. *Lawrence's Bestiary*. The Hague: Mouton, 1971.

Irvine, Peter L. and Kiley, Anne, eds. "D. H. Lawrence and F. L.: Letters to Dorothy Brett," *D. H. Lawrence Review* vol. 9 no. 1 (1976): 1-116.

Janik, Del Ivan. "The Unity of *Last Poems.*" *Texas Studies in Language and Literature* vol. 16, no. 4, 1975.

Kermode, Frank. *The Sense of an Ending: Studies in the Theory of Fiction.* London: Oxford University Press, 1968.

———. "Lawrence and the Apocalyptic Types." *D. H. Lawrence: The Rainbow and Women in Love*, edited by Colin Clarke. Nashville, London: Aurora Publishers, 1970.

———. *D. H. Lawrence.* New York, N.Y.: Viking, 1973.

Kirkham, Michael. "D. H. Lawrence's *Last Poems.*" *The D. H. Lawrence Review* vol. 5, no. 2 (1972): 197-220.

Klassen, William "Vengeance in the Apocalypse of John." *The Catholic Biblical Quarterly* vol. 28 (1966): 300-11.

Krishnamurti, M. G. *D. H. Lawrence: Tale as a Medium.* Mysore: Rao and Raghaven, 1970.

Kübler-Ross, Elisabeth. *On Death and Dying.* New York: MacMillan, 1970.

Lawrence, D. H. *Movements in European History.* London: Oxford University Press, 1925.

———. *Selected Essays.* Harmondsworth, England: Penguin, 1950.

———. *Studies in Classic American Literature.* Garden City, N.Y.: Doubleday, 1953.

———. *Apocalypse.* New York, N.Y.: Viking Press, 1960.

———. *Fantasia of the Unconscious.* New York: Viking Press, 1960.

———. *Collected Letters.* 2 vols. New York: Viking Press, 1962.

———. "*Women in Love* and Death." In *D. H. Lawrence: A Collection of Critical Essays*, edited by Mark Spilka. Englewood Cliffs, N.J.: Prentice-Hall, 1963.

———. *Complete Poems of D. H. Lawrence.* New York, N.Y.: Viking Press, 1964.

———. *The Symbolic Meaning. The Uncollected Versions of Studies in Classic American Literature.* New York: Viking Press, 1964.

———. *Lady Chatterley's Lover.* New York: Bantam, 1968.

———. *The Virgin and the Gipsy.* New York: Bantam, 1968.

———. *Lawrence & Italy: Twilight in Italy, Sea and Sardinia, Etruscan Places.* New York: Viking Press, 1972.

———. *Phoenix: The Posthumous Papers of D. H. Lawrence (1936).* New York: Viking Press, 1972.

———. *Psychoanalysis and the Unconscious and Fantasia of the Unconscious.* New York: Viking Press, 1972.

———. *St. Mawr and The Man Who Died*. New York: Random House, [n.d.]

Leavis, F. R. *D. H. Lawrence, Novelist*. New York: Simon & Schuster, 1969.

Levin, Harry. *The Myth of the Golden Age in the Renaissance*. Bloomington, Ind.: Indiana University Press, 1969.

Lifton, Jay, and Olson, Eric. *Living and Dying*. New York: Bantam, 1975.

Mannheim, Karl. *Ideology and Utopia*. New York: Harcourt, Brace, & World, 1964.

Marshall, Tom. *The Psychic Mariner*. New York: Viking Press, 1970.

Maupassant, Guy de. *Contes Choisis*. Garden City, N.Y.: Doubleday, 1961.

May, John R. *Towards a New Earth: Apocalypse in the American Novel*. Notre Dame, Ind.: Notre Dame University Press, 1972.

Miller, Madeleine S., and Miller, J. Lane. *Harper's Biblical Dictionary*. New York: Harper & Row, 1952.

Mommsen, Theodor. *The History of Rome*. 5 vols. Glencoe, Ill.: Free Press, [n.d.]

Moore, Harry T., ed. *Sex, Literature, and Censorship*. New York: Viking Press, 1953.

Morris, Tom. "On Etruscan Places." *Pauch* vol. 40-41, 1975.

Moynahan, Julian. *The Deed of Life: The Novels and Tales of D. H. Lawrence*. Princeton, N.J.: Princeton University Press, 1963.

Nehls, Edward, ed. *D. H. Lawrence: A Composite Biography*. 3 vols. Madison, Wis.: University of Wisconsin Press, 1959.

Nulle, Stebleton H. "D. H. Lawrence and the Fascist Movement" *The New Mexico Quarterly* (1940).

Pallotino, Massimo. *The Etruscans*. Harmondsworth, England: Penguin Books, 1955.

Panichas, George A. *Adventure in Consciousness: Th Meaning of D. H. Lawrence's Religious Quest*. The Hague: Mouton, 1964.

Pritchard, R. E. *D. H. Lawrence: Body of Darkness*. Pittsburgh, Pa.: University of Pittsburgh Press, 1971.

Pryse, James. *The Apocalypse Unsealed: Being an Esoteric Interpretation of the Initiation of Iahannes*. Los Angeles, Calif.: Pryse, 1925.

Randall-MacIver, D. *The Etruscans*. Oxford: Oxford University Press, 1927.

Selected Bibliography

Rexroth, Kenneth. *An Autobiographical Novel.* Garden City, N.Y.: Doubleday, 1966.

Richards, Hubert J. *What the Spirit Says to the Churches: A Key to the Apocalypse of John.* New York: P. J. Kennedy, 1967.

Richardson, Emeline. *The Etruscans: Their Art and Civilization.* Chicago: University of Chicago Press, 1964.

Russell, Bertrand. *The History of Western Philosophy.* New York, N.Y.: Simon and Schuster, 1945.

———. *The Autobiography of Bertrand Russell: The Middle Years, 1914-1945.* New York: Bantam, 1969.

Russi, Mathias. *Time and History: A Study of the Revelation.* Richmond, Va.: John Knox Press, 1966.

Sagar, Keith. *The Art of D. H. Lawrence.* London: Cambridge University Press, 1966.

Sale, Roger. *Modern Heroism: Essays on D. H. Lawrence, William Empson, and J. R. R. Tolkien.* Berkeley, Calif.: University of California Press, 1973.

Shneidman, Edwin. *Deaths of Man.* Baltimore, Md.: Penguin Books, 1974.

Schorer, Mark. *D. H. Lawrence.* New York: Dell, 1968.

Scullard, H. H. *The Etruscan Cities and Rome.* New York: Viking Press, 1967.

Seltman, Charles. *Women in Antiquity.* London: Pan Books, 1956.

Spark, Muriel. *Memento Mori.* London: MacMillan, 1959.

Spender, Stephen, ed. *D. H. Lawrence: Novelist, Poet, Prophet.* New York, N.Y.: Harper and Row, 1973.

Spears, Monroe K. *Dionysus and the City.* Chicago: University of Chicago Press, 1962.

Spilka, Mark. *The Love Ethic of D. H. Lawrence.* Bloomington, Ind.: Indiana University Press, 1955.

Springer, Mary Doyle. *Forms of the Modern Novella.* Chicago, Ill.: University of Chicago Press, 1975.

Stoneburner, Tony. Notes on Prophecy and Apocalypse in a Time of Anarchy and Revolution: A Trying Out. In *Literature and Revolution,* edited by George White and Charles Neuman. New York: Holt, Rinehart & Winston, 1972.

Taubes, Jacob. "From Cult to Culture." *Partisan Review* vol. 21, no. 4, 1954.

Tedlock, E. W., Jr. *D. H. Lawrence and "Sons and Lovers": Sources and Criticisms.* New York: New York University Press, 1965.

Tindall, William Y. *D. H. Lawrence and Susan His Cow.* New

York: Columbia University Press, 1939.

———. *The Later D. H. Lawrence.* New York: Columbia University Press, 1939.

Torrey, Charles C. *The Apocalypse of John.* New Haven, Conn.: Yale University Press, 1958.

Trilling, Lionel. *Sincerity and Authenticity.* Cambridge, Mass.: Harvard University Press, 1972.

Vickery, John B. Myth and Ritual in the Shorter Fiction of D. H. Lawrence. *Modern Fiction Studies* vol. 5, 1959-60.

Weiner, Ronald S. "The Rhetoric of Travel; the example of *Sea and Sardinia.*" *D. H. Lawrence Review* vol. 2, no. 3, 1969.

Widmer, Kingsley. *The Art of Perversity: D. H. Lawrence's Shorter Fictions.* Seattle, Wash.: University of Washington Press, 1962.

Williams, Raymond. *Culture and Society, 1780-1950.* Garden City, N.Y.: Doubleday Books, 1960.

Willard, James. *The Search for the Etruscans.* New York: Saturday Review Press, 1973.

INDEX

Anaxagoras, 146
Anaximander, 74, 145-46
Anaximenes, 73, 146
Apocalypse. See Lawrence, David Herbert, *Apocalypse*
Apocalyptic. See Lawrence, David Herbert, *Apocalypse*
Athanaeus, 75-76

Baker, James R., 171 n6
Barti, Luisa, 85
Bentley, Eric, 167 n33
Bismarck, 31
Bloch, Raymond, 71-72, 108-10
Blood consciousness, 33, 97, 125, 140. See also Lawrence, David Herbert, *Apocalypse; Etruscan Places*
Brewster, Earl, 79
Brown, Norman O., 160. *Life Against Death*, 37, *Love's Body*, 28, 36, 37
Burnet, John, *Early Greek Philosophy*, 73, 145-46
Burrell, Rose Marie, *A Catalog of D. H. Lawrence's Reading from Early Childhood*, 61

Campbell, Joseph, 18
Carossa, Hans, 70
Carter, Frederick, *The Dragon of the Apocalypse*, 137-38
Cassirer, Ernst, 169
Cavitch, David, 18, 19
Charles, R. H., 131
Christ, 39, 69; phallic Christ, 69. See also Lawrence, David Herbert, *Apocalypse, The Man Who Died*

Cipolla, Elizabeth, 128 n2
Clark, L. D., 16, 164 n1, 165 n23
Clarke, Colin, *River of Dissolution: D. H. Lawrence and English Romanticism*, 27, 52
Cles-Reden, Sibylle von, 76, 81
Cohn, Norman, *The Pursuit of the Millenium*, 134-37, 157, 160
Comedy. See Lawrence, David Herbert, *The Virgin and the Gipsy*
Consciousness. See Lawrence, David Herbert, *Apocalypse*, mind, pre-cognitive
Cowan, James C., 17, 18, 19, 165 n17

Death, biological, 21, 50
Death-in-life, 20, 24, 30, 31, 32, 123
Dennis, George, *The Cities and Cemeteries of Etruria*, 77-78
"D. H. Lawrence and the Fascist Movement," 167 n33
Dissolution, 27, 52
Domination, 40
Donoghue, Denis, 167 n38
Dostoievski, Fyodor, 41, 95

Engels, Friedrich, 135-36, 154, 160
Eschatology. See Lawrence, David Herbert, *Apocalypse*
Etruscans, 22. See also Lawrence, David Herbert, *Apocalypse*

Farrar, Austin, 130-31
Ford, George H., 16
Frankfurt, Henri, 85, 86
Freud, Sigmund, 145; *Civilization and Its Discontents*, 112
Frye, Northrop, 56, 165

179

Gibbon, Edward, *The Decline and Fall of the Roman Empire*, 114, 152
Gilbert, Sandra, 128 n1, 166 n28
Golden Age, 68-113, 145. *See also* Lawrence, David Herbert, *Etruscan Places*
Goodheart, Eugene, 162; *The Utopian Vision of D. H. Lawrence*, 138
Goodman, Paul, and Percival, *Communitas*, 102
Gregory, Horace, 155
Guthrie, W. K. C., 74, 166 n24

Hassall, Christopher, 68-69
Hencken, Hugh, 77
Heraclitus, 73, 74
Heurgon, Jacques, 107
Hochman, Baruch, 112; *Another Ego*, 155
Hus, Alain, 76, 99
Huxley, Aldous, 16
Hylozoism, 73

Incarnation, 29, 36-38
Inniss, Kenneth, *Lawrence's Bestiary*, 89
Intuition, 42

John of Patmos. *See* Lawrence, David Herbert, *Apocalypse*
John, St.
Jung, Carl, 112

Kafka, Franz, 152
Keats, John, "Ode to a Nightingale," 52
Kermode, Frank, 26, 132-33, 142, 155-56
Kirkham, Michael, 128 n3
Klassen, William, 166 n26

Lapsing out, 29, 31, 45-46
Lawrence, David Herbert: dark gods, 51, 53, 58, 100; death, near, 21, 50, 70, 128 nl, 169 *Apocalypse*, 18, 20, 21, 22, 23, 41, 43, 73-74, 129-164; antiapocalyptic, 156-60; beginnings, theory of, 132, 159-60; blood consciousness, 140, 163; Buchenwald, 150; Burnet, John, *Early Greek Philosophy*, 145-46; Christ, Jesus, 147-49, 153, 154, 155; cultism, 141, 165 n19; Dachau, 150; *Daniel, Book of*, 134; elitism, Lawrentian, 147-49, 152-56, 163; endings, theory of, 132, 142-43, 159-60; esthetic, Symbolist, 143, 147, 163; fictions, theory, 132, 142; hylozoism, 138-41, 165 n16, 166 n24; individualism, 163; Joachim of Fiore, 157; Joachitism, 157-58, 167 n37; John, St., 130, 131, 133, 134, 144, 147-55, 163-64; messianism, 134-37; mind, precognitive, 138-47, 163-64; Old World sensibility, 138-47, 158-59, 161 n38; power, 155; pre-Socratic philosophers, 145-47; Rananim, 161; regeneration, 160-62; *Revelation, Book of*, 148-54, 160-62, 166 n26; revolution, 160-62; *theos*, 144, 166 n24
"A Propos of *Lady Chatterley's Lover*," 19, 20, 42, 46-47
Etruscan Places, 18, 20, 21, 22, 23, 68-117; antianthropomorphism, 83-84; Arcadia, 113; archaeologists, 103-04; art, mortuary, Etruscan, 80, 83, 89-91, 100; Babylonians, 73; becoming, ideal of, 95-96; Caere, (Cerveteri), 71, 79, 80, 101; *Cippi*, 72, 100; class-structure, Etruscan, 94, 95; consciousness, mental, 101; death, 104; demoracy, 96-97;

Disciplina Etrusca, 110; divination, Etruscan, 108-10; Egyptians, 73; elitism, Lawrence's, 95-96; esthetic, Etruscan, 105, 106, 108; esthetic, Lawrence's, 105; esthetic, Symbolist, 82, 110, 117 n58. *See also* Lawrence, David Herbert, *Apocalypse*; esthetic, Wagnerian, 105; Etruscan language, 85; Etruscology, 71, 73, 74; Fascism, 91-92; hylozoism, 73, 74; imperialism, Etruscan, 93, 116 n38; individualism, 112; I-Thou, 86, 107; *Lucomones*, 94-95; museums, 101-02, 103-04; Mussolini, Benito, 91-92, 98, 116 n45; objectivity, historical, 74; Old World sensibility, 73, 82, 84, 87-89, 109; phallicism, 99-100, 101; philosophers, pre-Socratic, 73, 74; place, sense of, 70, 104; power, 81, 89-98, 116 n39; primitivism, 86; religion, 83-84; Romans 69, 75, 90, 94-98; self, concept of, 111-12; sexual intercourse, 105-07; sexual symbols, 80; ship of death, 80; slavecamps, Etruscan, 107; Tarquinia, 77; Tarquinian tombs, 89-90, 101-02, 108; tenderness, 105-07; *theos* (god), 74. *See also* Lawrence, David Herbert, *Apocalypse*; totalitarianism in Lawrence, 112; touch, 105-07; vitalism, 98, 111; Volterra, 91-92; Volterran tombs, 103

Fantasia of the Unconscious, 81-82

The Flying Fish, 17, 19, 20

"Introduction to His Paintings," 19, 20, 41-42

Lady Chatterley's Lover, 18, 19, 20, 28, 41, 105-06, 168-69

Last Poems, 18, 20, 22, 24, 43, 69, 87-89, 118-28, 168, death-in-life, 123; mechanization, 120; nature, 126; selfishness, 118; selflessness, 118; "Abysmal Immortality," 120; "All Soul's Day," 124; "Bavarian Gentians," 124; "The Breath of Life," 118; "Death is Not Evil, Evil is Mechanical," 121, 122; "Demiurge," 118; "Difficult Death," 124; "Doors," 124; "Evil Is Homeless," 118, 120, 122; "The Evil World Soul," 122, 123; "The Four," 118; "Kissing and Horrid Strife," 123; "Mechanical," 122; "The Ship of Death," 125-28; "Strife," 122; "The Wandering Cosmos," 119, 122, 123; "What Then Is Evil?," 123; "When Satan Fell," 124

"Love on the Farm," 43-45

"Mana from the Sea," 87-89

The Man Who Died, 18, 19, 20, 21, 28, 39-40, 69

Movements in European History, 157

Oblivion Poems, 48-53, 124-28

Pansies, 19

The Plumed Serpent, 18

"Pornography and Obscenity," 19, 20, 42

"Preface to the American Edition of *New Poems*," 105

The Princess, 18

The Rainbow, 28, 34-36

"Resurrection," 15

"The Risen Lord," 37

St. Mawr, 18, 158

"Shadows," 46-53, dialectic in, 48-49

"The Ship of Death," 32, 43, 45-49, 69, 80, 124-28, 142

Sons and Lovers, 16, 28, 33-34

Studies in Classic American

Literature, 158
The Symbolic Meaning: the Uncollected Versions of Studies in Classic American Literature, 138-39
Twilight in Italy, 32
The Virgin and the Gipsy, 18, 20, 22, 55-66; apocalypse in, 67; communal inclusion in, 65-66; La Grenouillère, 61, 62; literary analogues in, 56, 60-65; Maupassant, Guy de, *Yvette*, 61-62; *Mother Goose*, 60; rebirth in, 26 n14; Tennyson, Alfred Lord, "The Lady of Shalott," 62-65; virginity, 61
"Why the Novel Matters," 38
The Woman Who Rode Away, 18
Women in Love, 16, 27, 29-31, 96-97, 157-58
Leavis, F. R., 55
Longville, Timothy, 171n 6

Malory, Thomas L., *Morte d'Arthur*, 63
Marshall, Tom, 128 n1
May, John R., 132-33, 161
Mechanization, 31
Melville, Herman, *Moby Dick*, 158, 163
Menandrine New Comedy, 59
Messianism, 39. See also Lawrence, David Herbert, *Apocalypse*, messianism
Mommsen, Theodor, 74-75
Moynahan, Julian, 55, 61
Mysticism, nature, 51

Nahal, Chaman, 168
Nature, 33-34, 43-47, 50, 51, 52, 87, 126
Nietzsche, Friedrich, 166 n27
Nulle, Stebleton H., 167 n33

O'Connor, Frank, 97

Pallotino Massimo, 77, 83, 85, 93, 108
Primitivism 86, 169, 170. See also Lawrence, David Herbert, *Etruscan Places*, primitivism
Pritchard, R. E., *D. H. Lawrence: Body of Darkness*, 67 n7, 69, 117 n58, 145

Randall-MacIver, David, 101
Resurrection, 28, 36. See also incarnation
Rexroth, Kenneth, 96
Richards, Hubert, J., 132
Richardson Emeline, 85
Rilke, Rainer Maria, 169
Romans, 22. See also Lawrence, David Herbert, *Etruscan Places*
Russell, Bertrand, 74, 104

Schorer, Mark, 29
Scullard, H. H., 110
Shneidman, Edwin S., *Deaths of Man*, 21
Shaw, George Bernard, 75
Spilka, Mark, 117
Symbolism. See Lawrence, David Herbert, *Apocalypse*, esthetic, Symbolist; *Etruscan Places*, esthetic, Symbolist
Syphilis, 41-42

Taubes, Jacob, 165 n19
Thanatology, 21
Tindall, William York, 117 n58, *D. H. Lawrence and Susan His Cow*, 165 n23
Transvaluation, 28, 62
Trilling, Lionel, 111-12

Unconscious, the. See Lawrence, David Herbert, *Apocalypse*, mind, pre-cognitive

Vickery, John B., 55
Virginity, 61. See also Lawrence, David Herbert, *The Virgin and*

the Gipsy
Vitalism, 34, 57, 83, 86, 98, 111. *See also* Lawrence, David Herbert, *Etruscan Places*

Wagner, Richard, 105
Wells, H. G., *The Outline of History*, 84
Whitman, Walt, 111

Widmer, Kingsley, 26 n14, 167 n36, 171 n6
Williams, Raymond, 112
Wilson, John, 86
Wordsworth, William, 111

Yeats, William Butler, 155-56